DENMARK
THE COÖPERATIVE
WAY

BY FREDERIC C. HOWE

Photo: Jonals Co. Copenhagen.

The "Meat-town" in Copenhagen

DENMARK
THE COÖPERATIVE WAY

BY
FREDERIC C. HOWE

COWARD-McCANN, INC.
New York

CONTENTS

v

174467

vi CONTENTS

PREFACE

As I reread the pages which follow I see that this is something more than the story of the coöperative movement. It is the story of an unfettered people; unfettered in that they can do anything they will without let or hindrance by any one but themselves. Important as the coöperative movement is, an unfettered people and a people which trusts itself to freely use its freedom is much more important.

Quite as important, Denmark has provided her people with implements to give effect to this freedom. They are both economic and political. They are of the simplest and most inclusive kind. Through them her people are endowed with means for the direct and mandatory expression of their will. From the bottom to the top, from the town councils to the nation at large, there is complete freedom to write what the people will into the laws of the land and to provide as they will for carrying such laws into execution. Not only are there no constitutional restraints on legislative action, there has been provided a system of proportional representation by which the composite will of the people is reflected in the parliament and the town councils. Even the local authorities are endowed with power limited only by the wish of the people. In Denmark we have a state that is free to go wrong if it will, but, and this is the important thing, it can go right if it will.

Growing out of this freedom is an expansion of the state into many fields of an industrial and profit-making sort. These activities are both coöperative and public. They have changed the state from a mere political agency into a suggestion of a freely operating coöperative association of the most democratic sort.

Of all these implements, the coöperative movement is the most significant. And it is as pervasive as the state itself. It is found in every village, as it is related to all of the more important activities of the nation. It enlists the humblest citizen on a plane of equality with the richest and transfers to those who produce and those who consume many of the activities which in other countries are performed by distant, if not hostile agencies, indifferent to the effect of their acts on the well-being of the people whom they profess to serve.

It is as a means to an end rather than as an end in itself that the coöperative movement is most important. It is the economic equivalent of political democracy, with which it goes hand in hand. One relates to the day to day interests, activities and life of the people; the other relates to those services where voluntary association necessarily ends.

Herein are the fundamental differences between this little democracy and our own. In place of trust in ourselves we have distrust; in place of self-confidence we have the reverse. Instead of simple, direct and easily operating political agencies we have limitations and legislative confusion, if not all but complete impotence.

It is necessary, I think, for the state to be endowed with these freely acting economic and political agencies. The modern state must be an economic thing, owning things and performing services that awaken community concern rather than the dissension which seems to inhere in the purely political State.

I have seen this awakening of interest in the cities of England by the taking on of burdens and especially by the ownership of such things as water works, electric light works, gas works, tramways, housing, and other services which progressively distinguish the city of today from the city of forty years ago. I have noted the aroused interest of business and professional men in public affairs and the eagerness with which men of distinction sought for place on the town council and served with pride on those major committees that deal with transportation, gas and electricity and housing. Not only were the cities cleansed of the corrupting influence of these agencies when outside of the cities' life, but the city itself became the most dignified of all businesses in the community. As such it drew men of ability to its service, much as our colleges and universities, our hospitals, libraries and private clubs draw to themselves men who are exiled from political life by reason of their private business affiliations.

As I reflect on these things and especially as I observe the relations of the people of Denmark to their coöperative undertakings, I am led to wonder whether the failures of democracy in America are not in large part due to the relative emptiness of our political life, to its lack of a day to day contact with the people, and whether the divorce of the state from the ownership of things is not one of the real explanations of our failures.

With us the political State is at best but a secondary concern even to the most public-spirited citizen. Only at intervals does it make demands upon us. Its contacts are relatively unimportant. Impressed as our political life is by the *laissez faire* philosophy of England, the state has become primarily a policing agency, touching its citizens in the negative if not minatory way, and avowedly denying any collective participation of the people in the economic life of the community. Such remnants of social usefulness as this philosophy permitted to us have been largely taken away by the action of the courts. In consequence our major interests are almost wholly outside of the state. There is little left to draw men into political life as there is little left to create affec-

tion. As compared with Denmark the American State
is a limping, halting thing. It has itself invited those
failures which we attribute to democracy. Not only
have we violated our natural instincts for social rela-
tionships, we have transferred the major activities of
life almost exclusively into the hands of private enterprise if not of private exploitation.

Wherever one turns in the world today one sees
at bottom a struggle for power. This instinct may be
disguised by other avowals, but at bottom in every
country in Europe, and in America as well, the struggle is one for power. It may be for power in an individual; it may be for power in a class. This is as true
of labor as it is of capital. It is true of Denmark as
well. In Denmark, however, power is diffused. It is
possessed by the artisan in the city, by the agricultural worker, and by the peasant. It is lodged with
all of the people. And out of this diffusion of power
things have come of greater value than the mere
economic gains. There is a variety of interests, a
universal curiosity, and a richness of life, not to be
found in any other country with which I am familiar.
Those curiosities which in other countries are permitted only to the few are possessed by all classes
of people. Not alone as pertain to education, music
and art, but such as pertain to the curiosities which
spring from the doing of otherwise humble things.
Out of this diffusion of power and its long enjoyment has come a concept of human rights, of rights

as to life, as to all those opportunities which civilization offers to the world.

We experienced something of this sort during the Great War. It released something within even the individualistic American that he had never experienced before. And when the war came to an end we were let down into a far less exciting existence. All of us know scores of men and women who when the Armistice came went back to their work, to their profession, or to the home with an acute sense of loss in life. Latent powers and latent hungers were laid away, no longer to be used. We shrunk into a lesser stature. The political State said, in effect, that these instincts and these emotions must die for the time being until another war called them into action.

In Denmark the coöperative movement permits of a continuing peace-time outlet for these instincts. And it is this merging of many people in the doing of things together, and in the heightened values which come from the working together of men and women about a common objective that is significant. It is this, to me at least, that makes the coöperative way and the democratic way so much to be preferred to the socialistic state, no matter what its achievements may be.

I think it was this that the Secretary of Agriculture, Henry A. Wallace, had in mind when he said that "the hereditary nature of man is as well adapted to one order of society as another. In fact I am inclined to think that by nature most men are a little better adapted to the coöperative form of society than to the competitive." [1]

There is a final thing that Denmark has given to the world. And that is a rural civilization; a civilization which tomorrow may be as complete and rich in its possibilities as that which today finds its center in the city. It may be that we are approaching the end of that exclusively urban age which for us is six centuries long. And Denmark almost alone in the world has carried out to the land and to the people on the land those services and amenities which in other countries have remained almost exclusively the possession of those who live under city surroundings.

I doubt if I should have discovered these larger meanings of Denmark and the coöperative movement had it not been for long talks which I had in Washington some years ago when George W. Russell (Æ), the Irish poet and statesman, was in this country. To him the coöperative movement was a religion. To it he gave a great part of his life. In his "Co-operation and Nationality" I find the following confession of that religion, not for the Irish Free State alone, but for the world as well:

"Our co-operative associations in Ireland," he says, "gathering more and more into themselves the activities connected with production, consumption and distribution, and even in social activities, as they grow more comprehensive in their aims, make the individual more conscious year by year that his interests are identical with the

[1] "The Search For An American Way."

interests of the community. It is this spirit of mutual interdependence and comradeship in life, continually generated and maintained and inbred into the people, which is the foundation on which a great State, a great humanity, a beautiful civilization, can be built. The co-operative associations, properly constituted and organized, alone in modern times are capable of creating this spirit. Individualism in life or business can never create it. I never felt, so far, in any exposition of State Socialism which I have come across, that the writers had any understanding of social psychology, or by what means life may react on life so as to evoke brotherhood and public spirit. Understanding of economics apart from life there often was, and a passion for a mechanical justice, but I, at least, always feel that humanity under State control would be in a *cul de sac*. But it is quite possible to create without revolution, and by an orderly evolution of society within the State not controlled by the State, but finally controlling its necessary activities— a number of free associations of workers and producers which, in the country, would have been the character of small nations, and in the towns, of the ancient guilds, which would, I believe, produce more beauty, happiness and comfort than the gigantic mediocrity which always is the result of State activity.

"The Co-operative Commonwealth is the fourth alternative to State Socialism, the Servile State, or our present industrial anarchy; and Irishmen must make up their minds which of the four alternatives they prefer. They will be driven by the forces working in society to one or other of these courses. If capital wins we shall have the Servile State, and an immeasurable bureaucracy to keep the populace in order. If State Socialism wins humanity will have placed all its hopes on one system, and genius, temperament, passion, all the infinite variety of human

life, will be constrained by one policy. Our present system
is anarchic and inhuman, and the world is hurrying away
from it with disgust. The Co-operative Commonwealth
alone of all these systems allows freedom and solidarity.
It allows for personal genius and unhampered local initiative. It develops a true sense of citizenship among its
members. Whatever alternative Irishmen choose to promote they should think long and dispassionately on the
prospects for humanity which each offers, and consider
well their varying political, social and economic possibilities." [1]

This vision of a people living freely within the
political state is what the little country of Denmark
offers to the world. That it has been permitted to
go its way unhampered during the last fifty years
is of profound good fortune to western civilization.
That the adaptation of her democratic implements
to our own ends is possibly the most important obligation upon us I have no doubt. For without collective concern for implements with which to end the
conflict that prevails there is little of comfort or
hope in our present way of life.

Without shifting responsibility for any errors or
opinions which may appear in the text, I wish to
express my appreciation for the courtesy shown me
by the Danish Minister in Washington, Dr. Otto
Wadsted, and his associates; also to Dr. A. J. Poul-

[1] "Co-operation and Nationality," George W. Russell, published by Maunsel and Company, Dublin, 1912.

sen, Chief of the Danish Foreign Office Press Bureau,
Copenhagen. But most of all there is an impersonal
debt to the Danish people, among whom I moved in
the coöperatives, in the country, in the shops and
on the streets, from whom I got something which I
hope this book to some extent conveys, and that is
the impression of a people who have moved far away
from other peoples, with whom I am familiar, in
their way of living and thinking, in their generous
enlargement of human rights and in their feeling of
intellectual security as to what is fundamentally
sound, and in the dignity of the individual man and
woman and their rightful place in the state and in
the world.

I am also under obligation to Mr. Jacob Schalet
for help in the use of official reports, and especially
in the preparation of those parts of the book which
relate to the coöperative movement in America and
in other countries.

FREDERIC C. HOWE

Cosmos Club,
Washington, D. C.
October, 1936.

DENMARK
THE COÖPERATIVE
WAY

CHAPTER I

A LITERARY ADVENTURE
AND A DISCOVERY

I DISCOVERED Denmark quite by accident some fifteen years ago while writing a series of magazine articles on the post-war changes which were taking place in Europe. I was interested in things that governments were doing for people and in things that the people were doing for themselves. In a London hotel I had noticed strange markings on the shells of eggs served me at breakfast. As to why the shell of a hen's egg should have any mark upon it, I could not imagine. I sent for the head waiter and asked him about it. He said, "All of our eggs come from Denmark. Also all of our bacon. Danish eggs are strictly fresh. They are marked in that way to certify to their freshness. Danish bacon is the best in the world. It too is marked to certify its quality. If you want to learn more about it," he said, "you can do so by going down to the Danish Bacon Export Society in the old City of London close by the Bank of England. The farmers of Denmark," he continued, "manage all of these things for themselves.

1

They run their own business from the farm down to our hotel, down in fact to the consumers all over England. They pack and ship their products direct from the farm to their own selling agency in London, which in turn distributes them by trucks all over England. The farmers of Denmark are very much like an American trust.

"Everything is on the coöperative basis," he added. "The farmers save the profits which go to the middleman. And they insure goods of the highest quality, better than we can get from private dealers and better in fact than we can get from our own farmers here in England."

Why not "The Quest of a Hen's Egg" as a literary adventure? Possibly I could trace the eggshell from London back to the farm from which it came and see for myself how these farmers, up in the north of Europe, were running their own affairs, from the farmyard to the ultimate buyer, very much as the meat packing trust is run in America.

I crossed the English channel and the next day found myself in the City of Copenhagen, a city which I discovered to be one of the most beautiful in Europe. Not only beautiful, but apparently quite free from such evidences of poverty as I had left behind in the cities of England and on the Continent. Apparently there were no slums, no wretched tenements. The people too seemed different. There was a dignity and ease, a freedom of intercourse between men and women that was new to me. The cafés and restaurants were filled at all hours of the day. Across the public square from the beautiful Town Hall were the Tivoli Gardens where all classes spend their evenings, rubbing shoulders with one another in a democratic way, where all kinds of entertainment were offered without disorder, without vulgarity, and without confusion.

Had I found something bigger than a hen's egg, I wondered. Was this a little autocratic kingdom, with a capital made beautiful, as Paris was made beautiful by Louis XIV and kept beautiful to gratify his vanity, or was it something new and different in the world?

I called on the American Minister, Maurice F. Egan, whose enthusiasm for the people to whom he had been sent was as great as my curiosity as to the things I had seen. He aided me in meeting public officials. He provided me with an assistant who accompanied me about the city and into the country. He brought me into contact with the central offices of the Coöperative Wholesale in Copenhagen to aid me in finding the community from which the hen's egg had come and ultimately to find the neat little farm house, whose owner identified the markings on the shell.

Out of this visit I wrote a book entitled "Denmark: A Coöperative Commonwealth, Ruled by Farmers." The edition has been out of print for many years. With the recent rise in interest in the coöperative movement, requests have come to reprint

the book; to check over the impressions of 1920 and
see whether this experiment in democracy had continued to justify itself. This is the reason for this
book. It is substantially enlarged. For the most part
it is new, although the subject matter and the con-
clusions remain the same. The fundamental facts of
Denmark have not altered. Rather the movements
of fifteen years ago have strengthened themselves;
they have become permanent. In the intervening
period political power has been shifted further down
from the well-to-do farmers to the small scale
owner, the agricultural worker and the artisan class
in the cities, while the services rendered by the state
have been increased in number and strengthened
through the passing of farm tenancy, the wide-spread
ownership of the land and the universality of the
coöperative movement.

In the summer of 1935 I made an official trip to
Europe to learn what is being done as to the settlement of people on the land and the housing of people
by their governments. This study carried me to Ireland, England, Germany and Czechoslovakia, the
study being completed in Denmark, which country
has gone further in the resettlement of people on the
land, as with Sweden it has done more than any
other country in the field of coöperative housing.

What I discovered in 1935 was a different discovery from that of 1920. It was a discovery not of
coöperation so much, as of a democracy that had
issued out of the coöperative movement, out of the

ending of farm tenancy, and the various democratic contributions which the state has made to the well-being of the people. This new Denmark that I discovered was far more important than the coöperative movement; it was a discovery of something apart from physical things—something traceable to a new kind of liberty and a quality of freedom such as I had not found in any other quarter of the globe.

This book is an attempt to portray this democracy; a democracy that is spiritual as well as political; a democracy too that has been operative for nearly half a century and has developed an assurance and a technique that is, I think, of great value to the world.

CHAPTER II

A CHALLENGE TO CAPITAL-ISM, FASCISM AND COMMUNISM

DENMARK should be widely known about. It should be known about in America, to strengthen confidence in our institutions and in the possibility of working out our problems in our own traditional way.

For Denmark is a justification of democracy. It stands out from Fascist Italy and Nazi Germany, as it stands out from Communist Russia and capitalistic America. In the first place, Denmark has gone to the limit in democratizing its government. So complete is this process that the people seem to breathe through their government. It is part of their lives, as responsive to their orders as is the brain or hand of the human body. The Constitution, if such it may be termed, can be readily changed. It can be changed by an act of Parliament itself. And it changes from year to year. Not by action of the courts, for the courts are merely civil institutions

6

enjoying such limited civil and criminal jurisdiction as Parliament sees fit to bestow upon them. As in England, the Constitution adjusts itself to the changing needs of the day without cumbrous machinery of amendment. Nor is the Constitution a thing to be interpreted by the King or by the courts. Parliament is the sole judge of its own powers and when it decides a change should be made, its act is final.

Even in America, with the best of intentions, we find it difficult to admit of a society that might be better than that which we ourselves, or our class, controls. With us, the outposts of democracy are often of those who would see society altered in such a way that social minded persons would be entrusted with its direction and control. Even such an approach cannot carry us very far. Certainly it falls far short of what Denmark has brought into being. For Denmark is as free from the mere reformer motive of politics as she is free from control by privileged interests. Denmark is ruled, lock, stock and barrel by the people, by small-scale farmers, by agricultural workers and by wage workers in the city. The ruling group is not even the well-to-do farmer possessed of a medium-sized farm. It is a group coming from those who two generations ago were not greatly different from the serfs of continental Europe. It is this lowly peasant group that has carried democracy into all of the institutions of the country and made those institutions a mirror of the interest of all the people. And it is not that this class has power, it is the way it has used power and the undefinable something that has come from this use of power that is important.

Denmark has no fears of democracy. She has adopted the proportional representation system as to both parliamentary and local elections. Elections are made from large districts rather than a single one from lists made up of the outstanding men in the respective parties. The total vote cast by each party is apportioned so that it is reflected in the membership of Parliament. In consequence each party is represented according to its numerical voting strength. The result is that Parliament, and the town councils as well, are a cross section of the prevailing opinion of the country, as they are a cross-section of the relative strength of the various voting groups. Men no longer represent local constituencies. They represent the state as a whole. And they get into Parliament by having attained a national rather than a local distinction. There is little opportunity for local or special interests in such a system, as there is only the most limited possibilities for log-rolling or pork-barrel methods.

Year by year and decade by decade, this adjustment of the government to needs has been going on, until today, of the eleven members of the Ministry, all save three are social democrats, the remaining three being representative of left-wing opinion. With this change of political power, there has been a similar change in economic issues and in social legislation. The political state is a reflection of the economic state, while the economic state in turn is a reflection of the political state.

There are men in Denmark who are not content even with this extreme democracy. And one of the interesting things of this little country is the freedom with which men propose and discuss unusual political devices. Novelty is invited rather than the reverse. New suggestions make their way as they find adherents. Democracy in Denmark is much more than voting. It is something that is going on all the time, with the utmost freedom of discussion and the participation of all classes.

Along with this the political state has become frankly an economic implement, an implement to be used to better living in all its relations. It is not a distant, detached thing. While Fascism has merged the political state with capitalism and landlordism, Denmark has merged the political state with all the people, operating through the freest possible discussion.

Denmark is a contrast to socialism and communism no less than to capitalism. Covering a period of fifty years, the country has approached a cooperative commonwealth as it has developed an economic system not greatly different from socialism in its aims, but with a broad coöperative base and involving the continuous activity of the people. This has been done through the coöperative movement, a movement which calls into action the activity of an army of people rather than of a few. And this continuous contribution of many people is possibly of more real value than any economic contribution which could be made by any kind of socialized state. It has the qualities of a biological society; a society that is in a permanent ferment, bringing forth things of value to its members.

There are dangers from any society operated from the top, whether it be that of extreme capitalism, or of political socialism. In such a society the thinking is done by a few—by a few who have been placed in positions of power by accidental considerations. They are occupied with personal and political ambitions; with the confusion incident to a bureaucratic system. Even in a socialized state action has to make its way against obstructions; obstructions inherent in the system and possibly inherent in human nature.

Psychologically at least, both socialism and communism contain within themselves undemocratic elements which spring from entrusting power to a few persons; with endowing them with authority to do the thinking for the many. The coöperative movement is the reverse of this. It invites democratic processes; processes which approximate a natural order, in which men and women find their proper places and are free to contribute all they have to contribute; where they are in proper competition with others and are invited by the nature of the organization to contribute the best and the most progressive ideas of which they are capable.

Denmark is a much more conclusive exhibit of this today than fifteen years ago when I first visited the country. This is due in part to the training which thousands of men have received. It is due to the development of technique, of experience in working together. The shift of power downward from one class to another has added to the efficiency of the movement rather than the reverse. It has reached a point where all but a small percentage of the farmers are part of an advancing society in which the economic motives are merged with the cultural and the political.

Capitalistic society makes little provision for such contributions despite its professions of "rugged individualism." Rather it progressively denies such forces. To a lesser degree the same is true of socialism and communism. They too tend to centralization, to bureaucracy, to the encouragement of the autocratic rather than the democratic impulses of men.

There is no form of purely political organization of which this is not true. It is true because of the inherencies of human nature; inherencies which can only be controlled by complete responsibility to the individual, which those in power are disinclined to admit.

There is very little thought in the world today as to fundamental principles which should guide the political state; such fundamentals as are to be found

in the philosophy of Rousseau and Voltaire, of
Quesnay, Turgot and the Physiocrats; in the
writings of Thomas Jefferson. To these men the
political state was an enlargement of the individuals
that composed it. Denmark justifies this political
philosophy. It justifies it in its institutions, it
justifies it still more in the instinctive motives to
which it appeals and in the release of the resourcefulness of the individual man. And in a few years'
time, this confidence in the average man from whatever class he comes, has created an economic system
that is unique in the world. It has created something
even better in the soul of the people. It is the acceptance and successful working of this philosophy
that make Denmark the outstanding contribution
that it is.

The democracy of Denmark has discovered a way
by which the peasant and the worker may reach any
political heights the country may offer. She has
created a life that is rich in possibilities; a life in
which all classes think and act with an intellectual
freedom and an understanding relationship with one
another that is not unlike the relationship of bees
in a hive.

All this has been brought about in fifty years'
time. Not by revolution, but by education, by discussion, and by a propaganda which is welcomed by
the state and by public opinion. There is a continuing search for the next step, a step which
promises a better distribution of wealth, a more

abundant production of wealth, and a more generous life for all. Teachers teach what they believe. Editors write what they believe. The colleges and schools are tribunes of a new dispensation. While there are class differences, they are free from bitterness. There is a very general agreement as to the goal; differences relate rather to the road to be traveled.

This little democracy is moving toward a socialized society. The progress of socialism is evolutionary and moderate. It accepts the teachings of Karl Marx in theory but is free to depart from them. There is a surprising admixture of extreme individualism, of voluntary coöperation, and of state capitalism.

This experiment in progressive or eclectic socialism is the more remarkable because more than 95 per cent of the farmers own their farms in fee. Less than 5 per cent are tenants. We would not expect socialism to find a fertile field under such conditions. Moreover, Denmark is a poor country. It possesses few minerals, few forests, a none too kindly climate, and little in fact, save the land and eager labor from which to produce the wealth to be distributed. In consequence there is little waste. Every resource is utilized. There is a continuing increase in the output of the soil and along with it an improvement in the quality of products. All this is directed to the creation of the largest possible exchange value in farm products so that these products will buy the largest volume of other things which the people consume.

Along with this is a determined effort to see that the tribute taken from the people in the form of middlemen's charges and processing costs or by monopoly charges are kept at a minimum. The products of the farm are carried to the ultimate consumer in England, which is the chief market, even the trucks which traverse the roads of that country being owned and operated by the farmers themselves. Bacon, eggs and butter are produced and distributed in this way. This is one side of the picture. The reverse is a similar determination to buy as much as possible with the products of the land. This too is attained through coöperative agencies. First there are the coöperative retail outlets in the country, in the villages and in the towns. Along with this is the mass purchase of fertilizers, of seeds, of farm machinery and the like. Above these local agencies are a number of wholesale coöperatives owned and managed by the retail units. Above these wholesales again is an international coöperative which buys for Sweden and Norway as well as Denmark. Finally there are mills and factories owned by the consumers which still further cut out processing costs especially where the element of monopoly enters. Very much as the automobile industry, the steel trust or the harvester trust in America control every process and check it from the beginning to the end, so the 3,600,000 people of Denmark and especially the 206,000 farmers look upon their merchandising as a nationwide community monopoly by means of which every possible benefit will inure to the people.

Whereas in America the drift in the last generation has been to increase the number of persons engaged in the distribution of wealth and along with it a marked increase in the overhead costs of distribution, in Denmark the reverse is true. The overhead burden and the number of persons in the processing groups are being reduced while those that produce wealth tend to increase in number. Denmark is a producer's state but a producer's state that produces in order that it may consume.

In all these matters democracy is a kind of universal police force. It polices itself. It provides watchfully against waste as it insists on efficiency, on experts and on economies of all kinds. And as a result of the wide-spread training in accountancy, in banking and in business practices there is a high level of administration and executive ability which is found in all classes of the community.

Denmark is in fact the reverse of Germany and Italy on the one hand and of America on the other. It is the only country in which democracy is completely conscious of itself and is accepted and believed in by the people. It is a democracy, with but little more than a generation of experience as a guide. It is a democracy too of trust and confidence. In this again it is the antithesis of Germany and Italy and of America as well.

Denmark is a democracy which is in no sense

legalistic. It is a democracy which takes little thought of reverence for political traditions. It is a democracy which operates through a responsible ministry and that proceeds to put into effect the thoughtful decisions of the people as soon as they are registered at the polls.

Denmark exhibits the fact that in a real democracy all of the people must rise together. They must rise culturally no less than economically, socially no less than politically. And that is a task of the first magnitude. It is a task as to which we can only see a small part of the ultimate gains; gains which contribute as much to the rich as to the poor, gains that involve a generous art of living, in which the ruthlessness of the economic struggle is reduced to relatively harmless proportions. And today it may be said, as it is said "there is no class war in Denmark." It is further said "there is no poverty in Denmark." At least, there is none of that hopeless poverty found in other countries. This has come about as the result of fifty years of effort, during which time political power has shifted continuously downward until it rests today with all the people.

In the present bewildered world, with so many of our institutions being questioned, an exhibit of successful democracy, of how it came to be and what it has come to mean, is important. Especially is this so, when that exhibit is an exhibit of a whole people using the state for the common good. Denmark is an exhibit of this sort; an exhibit which should not be passed by lightly, even though Denmark is a little country. For Denmark teaches us that democracy is possible; that it need not be a discredited thing.

Even more important than democracy itself, is the disclosure of hidden talents within the average man, which when given an opportunity to play, achieve things as to which almost all of us have questions. Denmark has opened this unknown world up to us. It might have remained an unknown world were it not for an exhibit such as that which this little country offers.

CHAPTER III

DENMARK AND THE DANES

DENMARK is not much of a country measured by its size. It is about twice the size of Massachusetts, less than one-third the size of New York, and one-fourth the size of Iowa. The population is slightly above that of Indiana—3,600,000, of which 59 per cent live in towns and 41 per cent in the country. Not including North Sleswig the total area is 15,586 square miles. This is slightly more than the area of Holland. It is about 4,000 square miles more than the area of Belgium and about the same as the area of Switzerland. The state of Texas is big enough to envelop twenty countries the size of Denmark.

The population is relatively dense, being about 200 to the square mile. As compared with other countries, France has 191.19 persons to the square mile, Switzerland has 236.97, while Belgium has 671.69 persons per square mile.

It is generally assumed that Denmark is a country of farmers with few towns. This, however, is not true. In 1930, with a total population of 3,600,000, about 2,084,000 or 58 per cent of the people lived in towns or cities. All told there are 85 good sized communities in the country, of which thirteen have more than 15,000 people and seven more than 25,000. The population of the capital, Copenhagen, is 771,000.

The rural population proper numbers 1,466,000, having increased less than 6,000 in 10 years' time. During that period, however, the population of the towns and cities increased by approximately 280,000, the population of Copenhagen alone having increased by 70,000.

Thus it appears that Denmark has not escaped the drift of population to the city. Fifty years ago the urban population comprised only one-fourth of the population while today it comprises more than one-half.

Divided according to occupations there were in 1930, 337,500 persons designated as inactives; 216,700 as domestics and 206,500 in administrative occupations, art and science. Commerce and financial operations employed 386,200 and traffic and commission business 254,100. Industry provided employment for 1,032,300, while agriculture, forestry and fisheries together comprised 1,117,400.

Denmark consists of the peninsula of Jutland which obtrudes like a spike from the western corner of Germany and divides the North Sea from the Baltic. In addition there are three large and three small islands. Prior to 1864 Denmark included Sleswig and Holstein, two provinces to the south which

were absorbed by Prussia in that year. Of this territory, North Sleswig was returned to Denmark following the great war after a plebiscite in which
three-fourths of the inhabitants voted for reunion
with Denmark. North Sleswig has an area of 1,507
square miles, is one and one-half times the size of
Rhode Island, and has a population of 170,000. The
new "Greater Denmark" has a total area of 17,118
square miles.

Denmark's colonial possessions formerly consisted
of Greenland, Iceland and the Danish West Indies.
The latter were sold to the United States in 1916.
Iceland (area 40,000 square miles, population
90,000) which had enjoyed home rule since 1874 was
in 1918 voluntarily recognized as a free and independent nation by Denmark, the two countries only
being united by the same king. Greenland is now
Denmark's only colony. The Faroe Islands, which
also belong to Denmark, are not a colony but a part
of the kingdom.

Some years ago when Bertrand Russell was in
America he commented on our size and the problems
which size creates. These problems are in part geographical. They are in part political. They are also
social. They are problems involved in the making of
headway with the large amount of ballast which the
large country has to carry.

It may be that nations are too big. Certainly
many of our problems issue out of bigness. They are
problems not known to the smaller countries. It is

the big nations that waste themselves in wars, in armament races and in conflict over international affairs. Even the United States, protected as though we were a separate world, is spending for military purposes in excess of $1,000,000,000 a year. Compare this with little Denmark where almost the only issue that divides opinion is as to whether slight provision shall be made for defense or whether the army and the navy shall not be abolished altogether and where the total expenditure for military purposes is but 13% or $11,690,000 a year, about the budget of a good sized city in America.

In Denmark, one has a sense of awareness of everything that is going on. One is conscious of opinions, of movements, of varieties. In a little country it is easy to have a common objective. It is easy to convince a parliamentary group or even the voting population. Moreover, it is much easier for a man to be outstanding in a small country than in a large one and if he has pronounced opinions to impress those opinions on the nation.

This intimacy, efficiency and ease of life in the small country causes one to wonder why we should want bigness in a nation. From whence did this urge to widen our boundaries come and why do we hold to it with so much tenacity? Bigness generally is a survival of privileged power. For two thousand years it has been identified with the ambitions of rulers seeking military glory and personal distinction from great armies which the great state makes possible.

In our day the urge has been to exploit the outside world in the interest of imperialistic business. One wonders whether the gains from bigness equal the losses; as to whether the standardization of a continent under a single government is not to be regretted rather than the reverse. Would it not be better if the state were small and the government close to the people and reflective of their interest in an intimate neighborly way?

Whatever may be the gains and losses, the small countries of Europe have escaped many of the disasters of the greater powers. Moreover it is Ireland, Denmark, Sweden, Switzerland and Holland that are devoting themselves to social and cultural things and preparing the people to live rather than to die for their country.

It may be that it is inherently difficult for a small country to be militaristic if it is possessed of democratic institutions. Public opinion is sensitive. It makes itself felt as it cannot make itself felt in a large state.

And the people of Denmark are very close to everything that affects them. They are close to everything that goes on. Their close identification with the land contributes to this. They are in fact almost a part of the land.

A Danish writer tells of this identification. He says:

"Here on this peaceful spot of the earth has his

(the farmer's) family lived for as many years as he can trace. Ever since the thirteenth century has the church stood where it now stands ... for 700 years the voice of the bells has called from the church tower and sounded over the fields and meadows.... On the summit of the hill stands the windmill; its gray 'hat' and four wings stand out, a beautiful silhouette against the evening sky....

"Close by his own home the farmer can see other well built farms.... He knows many of their inhabitants. From the mound he can count six or seven church towers.

"What was he like, the old warrior who was buried in this barrow ages ago? It would be no real surprise to him, if he could come forth and see, what the country is like now, where once he and his kinsmen lived, fought and died. Would he know his descendants and approve of their work? But anyway, the farmer knows that he belongs to a race which through thousands of years has inhabited Denmark, cleared the woods, cultivated the soil, and been the founders of her culture....

"... the deep quiet feeling of belonging to the same family, the same race of men, who have lived here for more than a thousand years. This feeling tends to diminish the importance of the individual, but at the same time it places him as a link in an ever continuing chain. Here today, on this spot he has *his* work and *his* responsibilities just as some other day his son will have when his turn comes to take over the old farm. This is his home." [1]

Denmark is also one of the most unmixed countries of Europe so far as purity of race is concerned. During those centuries after the fall of Rome when conquering peoples were wandering over the face of Europe, Denmark was untouched by the southern and eastern races and remains today of the same ethnic stock as that which peopled the country before historic times.

These are facts to be borne in mind in understanding the achievements of the country.

As opposed to these advantages Denmark is a poor country. The land is low and for the most part flat. As compared with England, the climate is somewhat warmer in summer but colder in winter. There are heavy rain storms during a considerable portion of the year. The soil is far from fertile and up to a short time ago a large part of the peninsula of Jutland was barren heath of little value for agricultural purposes. Much of the waste lands have since been reclaimed and brought under culture by chemical treatment of the soil. There are no considerable rivers and few forests, only 8.3 per cent of the area being covered by trees.

The Danish people are related to the Swedes, the Norwegians and the English. In parts of the country the dialect spoken is understandable by an Englishman. The people are part of the old Norse stock.

[1] "Education in Denmark," Introduction pp. 5, 8.

Blue eyes and blond hair and complexions predominate. The religion is Protestant, the state church being Lutheran, to which nearly the whole population nominally belongs. The people are easy going and light hearted, though somewhat given to melancholy. They work hard, have a wonderful courage and tenacity of purpose, and great political aptitude, initiative and self-confidence.

There is little caste in Denmark. Birth or wealth count for little. Society is open to talent of any kind. There is little ostentation or display. The court life is simple. Members of the royal family move among the people in a democratic way. Not that the king is ignored. He is a very democratic minded and popular monarch, but the life of the people is so pervaded with democracy that display of any kind seems out of place. Hereditary titles are no longer bestowed by the Court, and the old nobility has ceased to exercise the political powers which obtain in other monarchical nations of Europe. The king advises rather than commands in legislation.

"National well-being is as common in Denmark as education," says Dr. Maurice F. Egan, the former American Minister. "Her people leave the game of international politics to others, but on the other hand they have a fine capacity for home activity and communal self-government, by which all the powers in a district work together for the development of local resources and are ready to adapt themselves to changing circumstances."

A British observer says: "The national characteristics of the Danish people are generosity, slowness
of speech; a good humor which has become
proverbial; determination almost amounting to
truculence, especially in the case of the peasants;
an immense capacity for hard work and sus-
tained effort; extreme democratic principles; a
strange fatalism which is a mixture of skepticism
and hesitation; and finally a complete and wonderful fearlessness in throwing over traditions
and prejudices." As to the great Danes, those
in power and authority, "they are neither great op-
timists nor extravagant idealists. Their dreams are
of a very practical nature and there is about them a
certain atmosphere of clean and sane humanitarian-
ism which is very attractive. They seem to carry out
their reforms in a spirit of common sense which is
almost scientific. Perhaps this is because their temperament is genuinely, rather than sentimentally,
democratic. They are a balanced people, their democracy is broad and practical, and the type is probably nearer English than any other on the continent." [1]

There is a generous hospitality and good-nature
on the part of the people. They give themselves
freely to leisurely living, to sports and entertainment
and especially to the bicycle. Life in Copenhagen is
not dissimilar to the life in the larger capitals on the
continent. The opera and the state-theater are sub-

[1] Denmark and the Danes, Harvey and Rupien, p. 26.

sidized and maintain a high standard of excellence. I have never been in a country in which the people participate more universally in all kinds of activities than in Denmark or in which they seem more generally free from care or concern for the morrow. This is true even in the poorer parts of Copenhagen, where the tenements are clean and orderly. If there are slums such as are to be found in New York and Chicago, London, Berlin, Paris or Vienna, I did not find them. In the provincial towns there is an appearance of well-being and equality.

The Danish farmer reads widely. And he supports many publications of an unusual sort. He will go miles to attend meetings. Education is a continuous process. And all kinds of educational agencies are a part of the farmers' daily life.

The art of Denmark is an art of peace and culture. One notes this in public places. The military hero is subordinate to the philosopher, to the artist, to the writer.

One gets the impression of wide-spread contentment; of a feeling on the part of the people that they enjoy all that the narrow resources of their country will permit; a feeling too that their government, their schools and the coöperative agencies which they themselves control, place the poorest farmer if not the worker in the city on a plane of equality, so far as many opportunities are concerned, with the rich land owner or with the city merchant.

The average peasant is informed on a great variety of subjects. He has well-defined notions on political questions and a remedy on hand for most of them. I have heard it said that the average farmer would go without his breakfast rather than his daily paper, and would walk for miles through the snow to attend a lecture. He is interested in politics, in history, in the traditions of his country. He is interested most of all in agriculture, in knowledge of the soil and of animals. He is a member of a number of coöperative organizations, he attends conventions and meetings of various kinds, and is identified with circles maintained in the schools and community halls by the state or one of the many organizations of which he is a member.

This is the estimate of the Danish peasant by scores of observers. Professor E. G. Cooley, writing of the culture of the Danish peasant, says:

"The Danish peasant is the best informed in the world. More and more class distinction is disappearing among them. They have lost the suspicious reserve of the usual peasant class. And not only among the peasants but among the working class there is not that chasm between the educated and the uneducated that is found among the other countries of the world." [1]

The Danes are liberal-minded in matters relating to marriage, divorce, the regulation of the social evil, in sex hygiene and matters involving personal liberty. Divorce is easy to obtain. If both parties re-

[1] "Educational Review," December, 1914.

quest it no misconduct on either side need be proved. There are a number of causes for judicial divorce, but divorces can be secured by agreement of the parties without other allegations. All that is required is that the contracting parties should appear before the proper magistrate. The judge frequently aims to bring about a reconciliation, but if reconciliation is impossible a decree of separation is ordered which becomes absolute at the end of three years, during which period neither of the parties can remarry. Mere incompatibility of temperament is sufficient cause of divorce. As a result there are no notorious trials, no baring of the personal lives of the parties and none of that sensational publicity that attaches to divorce in the United States and England. Apparently Denmark believes that liberty is preferable to either state or religious supervision of marital relations.

Women were granted the ballot in 1915 and have been admitted to office on the same basis as men, and their status seems to be one of complete equality in all the relations of life.

While all these things are true it is not to be assumed that Denmark is a little paradise. The people are not rich in the American estimate of wealth. There is not an automobile to every five persons. The wealth and well-being of the country is not to be measured by such standards. They are to be measured by the comforts, conveniences and opportunities which the great majority of the people enjoy.[1]

A man may have a small income, but if he is able to buy cheaply and sell advantageously, if he is protected from exploitation, if he is guarded in old age and sickness by insurance and given an opportunity to rise by his own efforts, he may be better off than the man with a much larger money income in another country. This is the kind of well-being that the Dane enjoys. The state is his state, the railways are his railways, education is designed to make life fuller and richer, while insurance, credit and other services are organized to serve the average man. Denmark is a nation of workers, of producers, and the life of the country is adjusted with the interest of these classes in view. Multi-millionaires do not exist. They do not seem to be necessary. The initi-

---

[1] A recent issue of "Danish Agriculture in 1935," published by the Agricultural Council of Denmark, exhibits the cash income of various types of farmers, the income being net income after allowances for all working costs and interest payments. It is as follows:

	1934-35		1933-34	
	per ha.	per farm	per ha.	per farm
	Kr.	Kr.	Kr.	Kr.
size of farm under				
10 ha.	230	1518	207	1366
10 to 50 ha..	88	2429	72	1987
over 50 ha. ..	25	2893	20	2316

(1, hectare = 2.47 acres)

From the above it appears that in the year 1935, a farm of under 25 acres had a net income of $410; a farm from 25 to 125 acres of $650; while farms over 125 acres had an average income of $782. Kroner—27 cents.

ative of the people has been awakened by other rewards than great wealth. And it finds ample opportunity to play through the thousands of coöperative societies, the educational institutions and the political activities in which the farmer and the worker take an active part.

Democracy in Denmark is far more than a form of government. It is a people, organized to use the government for the benefit of the people. It is economic rather than political democracy that distinguishes this little state from the other countries of the world.

All these gains have been achieved in little more than the lifetime of a single generation. They have been achieved without bloodshed or revolution. One abuse after another has been removed by legislation and by coöperative action, while the production of wealth has been increased and retained by the producers, until we have an incontestable exhibit of the fact that poverty, ignorance, insecurity, and fear can be ended in any state which really desires to end them.

CHAPTER IV

A PEACEFUL REVOLUTION

In the last quarter of the last century conditions in Denmark were not unlike conditions in America today. There was an all but complete economic collapse. It was primarily agricultural. As in America it was due in large part to an international situation which the people were helpless to control.

"The population," says J. J. Marais, the biographer of Bishop Grundtvig, "was slowly sinking into despair through economic as well as political disaster. Markets were closed. America from across the sea had become a competitor not to be despised. Germany had closed its door by a protective tariff. Floods, droughts, epidemics among cattle, plagues of all kinds swept across the country from time to time. What was to be done? How were the peasants to be heartened and kept to the soil? The Danes were inclined to 'Schwermunt' (melancholy). Were they to go under and become nationally and economically bankrupt? Were they to drift into towns and become hopelessly lost in purse and intelligence and more or less in spirituality?" [1]

In the middle of the last century the land of Denmark, like the rest of Europe, was largely divided among feudal landowners. Wheat and cattle were the major farm products. Intensive agriculture had not yet made its appearance. The "despair" of the people was largely due to the competition of the wheat fields of the American west, with their low cost of production. At the same time a prohibitive German tariff closed that country to Danish cattle. It was on these two products that the well-being of agriculture rested.

The collapse was more fundamental than this. Prior to the Napoleonic Wars, Denmark was a nation of substantial importance in the affairs of Europe. Alliances were sought with her by the greater powers. Norway formed part of the kingdom up to 1814, as did Sleswig-Holstein as late as 1864. The king made unfortunate alliances. The country sided with Napoleon and lost heavily as a consequence of his overthrow. The Danish fleet was destroyed in 1807 at the Battle of Copenhagen. By the Treaty of Kiel in 1814 Norway was taken from Denmark and united with Sweden as compensation for Finland which was taken from Sweden and joined to Russia. In 1864 Sleswig-Holstein was annexed to Germany. These were the largest of the Danish provinces.

[1] Bishop Grundtvig and The People's High Schools in Denmark.

As a result of these losses the population was reduced by one-third. The long wars with Napoleon had ruined trade. The debt of the country was heavy. The government was an absolute monarchy or "enlightened" despotism, the landed nobility filling the higher offices of the state. The peasantry was in a state of semi-serfdom, although the Scandinavian countries had always contained a substantial body of free peasant proprietors.

The tide began to turn in the seventies. It started with new ideas of education. It spread into social and political fields. The people ceased to concern themselves with foreign affairs and turned their thoughts to domestic problems. The phrase "outward loss, inward gain" became a working philosophy. This indifference to imperialistic adventures, to efforts to exploit other peoples, made an internal policy possible. Denmark now leaves the affairs of Europe to others. Her concern with the outside world is almost wholly commercial. The army and navy have been reduced to a skeleton police force. Today Denmark is practically unprotected from outside foes. She recognizes that complete protection is out of the question, and that the maintenance of a substantial military and naval establishment involves greater hazards than complete disarmament. She believes that there is a moral protection in complete disarmament; in complete unprotectedness.

The Dane also refused to emigrate in large numbers as did the peasants of other countries. Nor did he go to the cities. He did not demand a protective tariff to shield him from the competition of other countries. He did the reverse of all these things. He relied upon himself. And self-reliance is one of the characteristic qualities of the Dane. ↙

The Danish farmer abandoned the production of wheat and cattle and turned to small scale farming. From large scale agriculture he turned to dairying and butter and cheese making. He went into the raising of hogs and the production of bacon. He improved the quality of his butter and the quality of his bacon and created a foreign market based upon the superior quality of his products. The Danes did as to agriculture what England has done as to industry. They improved the grade of their products. Through persevering attention to details and the establishment of coöperative marketing and buying agencies, the Danes gradually won an uncontested place in the markets of England.

The change in the style of farming began about 1875. At that time England was buying her butter, eggs and bacon from Ireland. The Danes sent a commission to the latter country to learn how the Irish produced these things. Then they set to work to win the British market for themselves. Soon Denmark was producing better bacon, better butter, better eggs than the Irish. In recent years no less than four special commissions have been sent to Denmark from Ireland and Scotland to find out how it is done.

In fifty years' time the Danish peasant has become the most contented farmer in the world. The comforts and conveniences of life are widely distributed. The landed aristocracy has been reduced in number and power and many of their estates have been divided among the people. The important agencies of buying and selling are in the hands of the coöperative societies while the government has become a democratic agency working in the interest of the peasants and the workers. /

Prior to the great war Denmark was exporting food to England, Germany, South America and even to the Philippines. Since that time there have been recessions due to prohibitive tariffs and the depression. The following statistics indicate the growth of the export trade in farm products. Except for the years 1908 and 1931 the average is for a five-year period.

	AVERAGE EXPORT 1857-1879	AVERAGE 1895-1899	EXPORTS FOR 1908	EXPORTS FOR 1931
Horses	$1,750,000	$2,909,000	$3,200,000	$9,180,000 [1]
Cattle	5,250,000	3,000,000	7,000,000	
Bacon and lard, etc.	750,000	12,000,000	28,400,000	131,760,000
Butter and dairy products	6,500,000	30,000,000	49,150,000	106,380,000
Eggs	250,000	3,000,000	7,400,000	20,520,000
Total	$14,500,000	$50,909,000	$95,150,000	$267,840,000

From 1881 to 1912 the value of the exports of farm products rose from $25,500,000 to $150,000,000. In 1933 despite the depression and adverse tariffs

[1] Includes all live animals, except fish, etc.

they amounted to $220,600,000. Before the war most of the horses and cattle went to Germany. The bulk of the other exports went to England. The annual shipments to England alone amounted to nearly $90,000,000 of which more than one-half was in butter and dairy products while the balance was in bacon and eggs. Denmark still supplies Great Britain with these foods in spite of the greater area, higher fertility and greater natural advantages of the latter country.

The total export trade of Denmark in 1933 was $310,000,000 of which $220,600,000 was in six farm products amounting to approximately $1080 for every farm, of which 133,000 of the 206,000 are of less than 13½ acres in extent. The farm exports alone amount to $27.00 per acre in addition to the domestic consumption, as well as the support of the farmer himself.

The agricultural prosperity of Denmark is further indicated by the increase in live stock upon the farms. In 1881 there were 1,470,000 cattle. In 1914 the number had increased to 2,463,000 and in 1933 to 3,185,000. During the same period the number of hogs increased from 527,000 in 1881 to 2,497,000 in 1914 and 4,476,000 in 1933.

The average yield of butter of all Danish cows in 1864 was 80 pounds; in 1887 it was 116 pounds; in 1908, 220 pounds.[1]

---

[1] Coöperation in Danish Agriculture, Harold Faber, pp. 161-170, 1st ed.

This is merely the balance sheet of the country as expressed in increasing wealth and in export trade. It is a measure of recovery in money terms. Moreover this increasing wealth production has been accompanied by a better distribution of the wealth. It has gone to all classes. The gains have gone to the worker in the city and the farmer in the country. Wealth is more equitably distributed than in any other country in Europe; possibly more equitably than in any other country in the world.

The life of the artisan in the cities has been improved along with that of the farm. The average working class home is fitted with both electricity and gas, both of which are comparatively cheap. A good deal of electrical power is imported from the Swedish water power sources although there are in Denmark 456 power stations of which 276 are coöperatively owned.

Today measured by the well being of the people Denmark is one of the wealthy countries in the world. There is electricity and a telephone in nearly every farm house and upon all the coöperative premises. Many rural homes have central heating and almost all have their wireless or radio sets. The deposits in the savings banks amount to 2,200,000,-000 Kroner. 78 per cent of the savings banks are in rural districts. They are largely coöperative or mutual and are managed by the farmers.

The distinguishing thing about agriculture is the small size of the farms, many of them being of but few acres. Moreover there is no tenancy save as to a few small farms related to the large estates. This indicates the possibilities of farming under intensive cultivation when the farmer is protected from exploitation by the state and by his own coöperative efforts.

The coöperative movement began with dairying in the seventies and eighties and grew rapidly. During the next decade the farmers entered politics. By the end of the century the middle class farmers had risen to power in the Parliament. From this time on legislation was consciously in the interest of agriculture as in other countries it is in the interest of industry. Not only that, it was consciously in the interest of the peasants owning the small farm. Tenancy was seen to be bad. Cultivation was indifferent. The tenant had little interest in improving the property. He exhausted the soil. The farmers in and out of Parliament set to work to be rid of tenancy. They found that the farm tenant could not escape from his position without aid, for the large estate owners sought to keep him dependent upon them so that they could secure cheap labor. Moreover the tenant could buy a farm only on credit, while the landlords charged high prices for their land. To overcome these obstacles the government provided funds with which to aid the peasant to purchase the land at a proper price and by later legislation itself became the landlord. The would-be farmer became a tenant of the state which provided him with money to buy the land, to build a house and to equip the farm with cattle, machinery, tools, etc. The farmer himself was required to provide 10 per cent of the cost. He was given a long term of years in which to repay the debt. As a result of this and subsequent legislation farm tenancy has been reduced to 5 per cent of the total.

The farmers also impressed their needs on the railroads which are almost wholly owned by the state. Waste lands were opened up by the building of new lines. This developed new farms which were made available to owners. Passenger fares were reduced to encourage travel while freight rates were adjusted to enable the farmers to ship their products to England, and Germany as advantageously as possible.

Similar changes were made in the system of taxation while social legislation of the most advanced sort was provided for. As a result of these changes the farmers of Denmark have developed a civilization that is unique. Poverty has been greatly reduced. It has almost disappeared. The artisan has been protected by pensions, by insurance funds, by social legislation. In all of these fields the government has become a frank instrument for looking after the well-being of the people and for providing them with a sense of security and the fullest possible opportunity for individual initiative and resourcefulness.

The control of banking and credit is largely in the

hands of coöperative societies. The same is true of insurance and other farm activities. The farmer has become a business man, a banker, an insurance company, and a politician as well. These activities of the state have not produced an unreliant people. The reverse is true. The Dane is about the most self-reliant person in the world. And while he uses the state in many ways, he looks upon it as a means of insuring the largest possible liberty to the individual rather than the reverse. The Dane wants a free field and no favors. He believes in free trade. He has imposed taxes on wealth and on opportunity, rather than on thrift and consumption. He insists that the land shall be used by those best fitted to use it and that agriculture is best promoted through ownership, rather than through tenancy.

Denmark passed through a peaceful revolution in fifty years. This is the comment of all observers. "Denmark," says an English writer, "during the last half century, has been through the throes of a wonderful regeneration. Her peasantry has been emancipated from a condition of veritable serfdom; her education has been liberalized; her land system, agriculture and finance have been reorganized and brought to a pitch of excellence which is the envy of many a greater, less perfectly developed, state." [1]

Along with the emancipation of the serfs and the political ascendancy of the peasants, socialism has developed in the cities and towns and among the

[1] Denmark and the Danes, Harvey and Rupien, Foreword.

agricultural workers. The Social Democratic Party is now the largest party in the state. It is of the moderate, evolutionary type. It coöperates with other radical groups in legislation and administration.

CHAPTER V

A CONTRAST AND AN INQUIRY

COMING from the carefully manicured countryside of England one wonders why it is that Denmark should feed the British Isles. The people are of the same ethnic stock. The religion of the two countries is essentially the same. Nor is there any material difference in political institutions. Both countries are governed by a Parliament elected by popular suffrage, with a constitutional monarch, whose powers are limited but are substantially the same.

The climate of England is more favorable than that of Denmark. A great part of the land is fertile and can easily be made to produce more abundantly than the soil of Denmark. Yet it is devoted to grazing, to hunting and to pleasure instead of to producing crops which would raise the standard of living of her people far above what it is today.

England with four-fifths of her people living in cities, offers a food market of from twenty-five million to thirty-five million people. She could provide herself with vegetables and fruit, with eggs and butter, with cattle and dairy products. Yet she goes to Belgium for her vegetables, to Ireland for her cattle, and to the Danes for bacon, for eggs and for dairy products.

There are more striking contrasts. They relate to the life of the two peoples, to their culture, to the standard of living of the great mass of workers and farmers, to the disparity of classes. A large part of the English population is in extreme poverty; a poverty with little hope and little security beyond that which is provided by social legislation.

Denmark is a contrast as to all of these things. There is a sense of security on the part of all classes. And along with this, a social system which offers opportunities to the underprivileged to create a life of their own by easy access to the land, with protection to this life by a variety of agencies which the people themselves have created.

Why this difference between the two countries?

Why is it that people separated from one another by imaginary lines should differ so widely?

Why the difference between the French and the Italians; between the Germans and the Dutch?

Why have not the leveling forces of the last century eradicated such differences and brought people of the same climate and substantially the same conditions to equality in culture and economic well-being?

One cannot help wondering why it is that in a world in which unemployment has been continuous for half a dozen years, in which billions of dollars are being expended annually for relief, that statesmen, scientists and those who search the earth to add to human knowledge, do not make a study of a country like Denmark which has done so many things to offer a solution to these problems.

It would seem as though commissions would be created; that they would translate from nation to nation, the experiments people were making to escape from recurring depressions and especially from the poverty which everywhere goes hand in hand with civilization. Especially one wonders why the score of rich foundations of America, with tens of millions of funds, are not searching the face of the earth to learn how other countries are meeting these problems and solving them. For the last forty years, Denmark has been known as an outstanding exhibit of something not to be found elsewhere in the world. There have been some books on the subject; educators and experts have visited the country, yet we have less information as to Denmark than as to Central Africa.

There are a number of factors which explain why Denmark is different as to which all experts agree. These factors have different importance to different people. There are some who find the explanation in a great educator, in the life of Bishop Grundtvig, who more than a century ago gave himself to arousing the people, to creating a system of education and to altering the values which the people should place upon old and traditional things.

There are others who explain Denmark in her system of land tenure. To them the democracy of the country, the resourcefulness and widespread well-being of the people are to be found in the fact that the Danish farmer owns his own farm. He is no longer a tenant. He owes no obligations to any master. He works for himself. His rent is low rent; and it is fixed. It cannot be increased with every improvement which the farmer contributes to his holding. Here is a country in which 95% of the farmers are free, home-owning occupiers in which their homestead is their castle.

Universal land ownership creates a psychology that is far different from the psychology of the farm tenant of England, of the shiftless rack-rented cotter of Ireland in the last century, or of the share-croppers of the American south. There is something in working for one's self rather than for another that creates a revolution in one's thinking as it results in a revolution of one's relationship with one's fellows and with the state. In any country the farm tenant is at best but a qualified serf. He has no real freedom, social or political. He is tied to the land by his poverty. The harder he works the greater his fear of an increase in the rent he must pay for the privilege of living. Such fears are not found among the farmers of Denmark. Every gain they make, every improvement added to their farms, every con-

tribution of science or invention which they adopt
adds to their own well-being. It is not taken by the
owner in the form of rent for the right to use the
land.

Others find an explanation in the universality of
the coöperative movement. Not in a coöperative
movement like that of England, in which the savings of pennies in buying through a coöperative
store is the important thing, but in a coöperative
movement so pervasive and so woven into the life
of the people that it is little less than an industrial
system comparable to socialism.

The coöperative movement has passed out of the
purely economic stage and has become a training
agency of the first importance. It has educated the
peasant farmer in accounting and banking. It has
identified him with his village, then with the nation
and finally with the outside world. The management
of a local coöperative gave him confidence. Identification with a local credit union converted him into
a banker. The study of merchandising and the co-
operative purchase and sale of commodities made
of him an expert.

Whatever the major cause of the achievements of
this little country may be, all of these causes co-
operate in explaining it. They are woven into one
another. Education is related to the things men and
women do from hour to hour. It is related to the
farm, to the use of one's hands, as it is related to
the politics of the village and the state. It begins

in the elementary schools, but it is the adult school, the "People's High School" which is probably the most remarkable educational agency of the modern world.

Out of this merger of education, of the coöperative movement and of universal ownership, political democracy has emerged. It is a democracy which has all but ended classes and class strife. It has brought practically the entire adult population, women as well as men, into harmonious adjustment with a common political objective. There is little bitter party conflict such as is found elsewhere. The government in power as well as the opposition are divided on how best to do things rather than as to the class to be benefited.

These various forces within the community had a beginning. They did not come of their own volition. They are in large part the inspiration of a remarkable man, a man who in a larger country, would be accepted as one of the great men of his century. He was not a military leader, nor a statesman. He was a kind of social messiah with a passionate love of his country, of its people, and especially of the peasants. He was a spiritual agitator who paid the price of his agitation during his lifetime and who was not permitted to live to see the fruits of his efforts. Yet he vitalized the country. He gave it a spiritual and an economic formula; a formula that has persisted for a hundred years.

Whatever place may be given to the various economic forces, all observers agree that the beginning is to be found with Bishop N. F. S. Grundtvig, the spiritual father of Denmark.

CHAPTER VI

THE AWAKENING OF A
PEOPLE

On a low-lying hill on the outskirts of Copenhagen a great cathedral is rising. It may not be as large as the cathedral of Cologne but it gives the impression of being so. It is off by itself. It commands the surrounding landscape and is visible from the sea. The broad-faced tower with its vertical squared recesses rising like the pipes of an organ is obviously symbolic of Denmark. There is no touch of the artificial; only succession after succession of unadorned columns set up in mathematical array. The architecture issues out of something old. It gives the impression of being related to the distant past.

Round about the cathedral and enclosing the cathedral yard are low-lying brick houses for persons of modest means. They suggest the old houses which nestle around the cathedrals of the middle ages.

I was driving around Copenhagen and came upon the cathedral by chance. It arrested my attention. I did not know that people were building cathedrals in this age. And I hardly expected to find them being built in Denmark, where, however religious the people may be, they are essentially practical minded. I asked the driver to explain it. The cathedral, he said, was a monument to Bishop Grundtvig. It was not being built by Parliament, nor by the established church. It sprang out of the gratitude and affections of the people who are building it from their savings, not because they are called upon to do so but because they wanted to do so.

I, of course, knew about Bishop Grundtvig. I had found his name and his works recounted in every book on Denmark. I had found it in official reports. I had seen it identified first of all with education and then with almost every aspect of the present day life of the country. And so far as I know there is no other country, unless it be Russia, that identifies itself as completely and without reserve with a national hero as does Denmark. This hero is not a military leader; not a great statesman; but a priest, an agitator and a promoter of intellectual revolution. He was the spiritual father of the democracy of Denmark.

It is one thing to free a people from a foreign ruler as did Washington, as it is one thing to free an enslaved race as did Lincoln. It is another thing to free a people from themselves; to free them so completely that the powers that they individually possess are set at liberty. That, I think, is what Bishop N. F. S. Grundtvig did for Denmark.

"Outward loss, inward gain," is a phrase to be found in all books on Denmark. It is a phrase repeated by her teachers, statesmen, thinkers. To some this means a consolation to the people for the loss of Sleswig-Holstein in 1864. To others it means a consolation for the economic collapse due to the loss of foreign markets and the competition of the wheat fields of America. True the phrase means these things, but it means something far more important; something more significant than anything which other emancipators have given to their people. Within this phrase is to be found a mandate to the individual, more particularly to the peasant and the man farthest down, to have courage, intellectual integrity, spiritual sincerity, and to believe in himself and in his inherent right to want and think for himself.

Grundtvig, a Lutheran priest and late in life a bishop, wrought a profound change in the common people; in the peasants; even in those but a step above the medieval serf. He carried the motive of the Protestant Reformation to its depths and insisted on a conscious liberation of rights, economic, political, social and cultural.

This mandate to the peasants, for whom Grundtvig had a passion, released something within the soul of men and women, that is known to the Dane but which has been for the most part undiscovered by foreign observers.

One of the significant things about the democracy

of Denmark, is that all of the institutions are being carried up together. The cultural life is as high as the economic life. The physical well-being is paralleled with an intellectual well-being, while the distribution of the land and the coöperative movement go hand in hand with a democratization of the state.

Denmark is an exhibit of these fruits of democracy. They have sprung from the same roots and flowered at the same time and in much the same way. And decade by decade they have included an increasing number of people who share in a like degree in the life of the country and share in it as a matter of human right rather than as a gift from their betters.

While it would be incorrect to say that this is a gift from a single man, yet all Danes and all commentators on the Danes, trace the source of these things to Bishop Grundtvig, who, born in 1783, continued throughout his life, which came to an end in 1872, protesting against the medievalism of the old order and the rightfulness of something new.

Grundtvig came from an old Danish family. He received a conventional education and was trained for the ministry. He was a poet and a historian as well as a priest. Religion to him was of primary importance. He spent some time in England where he found the country in the throes of the struggle over the Reform bill and the political controversies of the early part of the last century. It was here that his idea of a new kind of education took form, as it was here that he came in touch with the new movements of the people.

Grundtvig was deeply versed in the folk-spirit of the old Norseman. And it appealed to him as something to be recalled and made a part of the life of the people. He felt that the age-long culture of his country should be a living reality. And one of his earliest writings, "A Scandinavian Mythology," (1808) was a portrayal of the life of the old Norseman as a struggle between mind and matter.

Grundtvig lived through the period of the Napoleonic Wars which had brought much misery to Denmark. He was familiar with the foreign influences that shaped the intellectual as well as the political life of the country. He was a great admirer of the English, and felt that he had found in their country the things that were stagnant in his own. "The English," he said, "are the best examples of Thor that we can show today." In the English he felt that the heroic forces of the gods of his own country had been released whereas at home they had been forgotten.

It is with education that the name of Grundtvig is most closely linked. Without the changes wrought in the education of the average man it is doubtful if any of the other revolutionary changes of Denmark would have come about. And no educator and few statesmen have as completely changed the destiny of their country as did this long neglected and bitterly reviled educator, whose protests against the prevailing system have lifted the peasantry of Denmark to a high level of culture. Education in turn has reacted on political and economic conditions. It is something which the peasant himself controls. It has penetrated down from one class to another until it has given a full rounded life to those at the bottom.

Grundtvig found the Danish language and Danish culture neglected in the schools, which were classical in the extreme. Latin and German were emphasized. He turned in disgust from the schools and termed them "The black school" or "The school of death." In their stead he sought to create "a school of life," "Where the mother tongue shall prevail," and where Danish culture was not to be a despised guest, but where the ancient traditions of the country were to be revered. He protested against the privileged character of education; an education designed for the leisure classes. 'Obviously," he said, "only the very few can and must be professors and learned folks at one time, but we must all be Danish citizens, enlightened and useful citizens."

Grundtvig urged "the education and enlightenment of all the people in contrast to erudition and declared that the school should be independent, complete in itself, not "a sort of preparation for erudition, so that it may not become an empty shadow but a real intellectual force, whereby life and the moment assert the right which the erudite are inclined to ignore but which are inalienable."

Back of his passion for a new type of school was a passion for the peasant. And it was to give dignity to the peasant, to awaken a pride in his calling no matter how humble it might be, that inspired his teaching. Grundtvig wanted to see the peasant and working man lifted from the dull soulless occupation to which they were condemned into something better. The schools were under foreign influence. As to the educated classes, "three-fourths of them," he said, "can hardly write Danish, know nothing of history . . . have no conception of civilization except as something dry and repulsive as necessary to be 'got up' for the examination."

Within this system he could see no hope for the people so long as they were dependent upon the cultural ideas of other nations and so long as education was dominated by the privileged classes. Denmark he felt would continue to decay unless these influences were arrested and a purely cultural society substituted in their stead. "What the peasants need," he said, "is not technical training but mental." Two of his principles were (1) that all traditional methods be discarded; and (2) that the national spirit be aroused. The highest in any human being is not brought out by examination; it must be aroused by something else. "Our primary aim is to inform, not to impart information," he said.

Grundtvig had no interest in any detailed course of study or curriculum. He said "that man must first be born before one can know what will suit him."

He laid down the principle that the purpose of the school was not to be text books or examinations but, "an enlightenment at the free option of all and containing its own reward." Text books and reading were to play a subordinate part. It was the spoken word, "the living word," borne by the force of personal conviction that was to be the bond between the teacher and pupil and to create an intellectual communion between them.

Any form of examination or test was anathema. Education came from the outstanding personality of the teacher. He was to be chosen because of his ability to inspire. The teacher must live and work with his pupils. He was to be the center of the school and of the community life within which the school was located. Through intimate connection with the pupil he would inspire them to belief in those things which are fundamental to real culture.

There were to be no separate class divisions in the schools. Knowledge was to be sought for its own value irrespective of its usefulness. J. J. Marais, the biographer of Grundtvig says: "No doubt every student at the end of his four or five months' course knows many things that he did not know before, but whether he knows many or a few things is a matter of small concern, so long as a new hope, a new life, a new spring of energy within him is called into being."

Throughout all his teachings there was a spiritual passion for everything that was Danish and especially for the people. And it is to be remembered that Grundtvig lived and did his teaching prior to the middle of the last century before such ideas had made their appearance in a great part of Europe. He was essentially a pioneer in his belief in people, in their capacities and especially in their right to live. "Our national culture," he said, "must rest upon the enlightenment of all classes. ... If education is organized as if every one were to be an officer or a gentleman of leisure, the entire people will die of hunger. It is not a question of what will be serviceable for the officials or leisure class, but for those who will be neither the one nor the other. Our aim must be to provide a liberal education which will make the whole people fit for their work and happy in their situation. ... The aim of the schools should be to fill the gap between the educated and the uneducated, to bridge the boundless abyss which the hierarchy, the aristocracy and the Latin schools have built between almost the entire people on the one side and the handful of the so-called educated and enlightened upon the other." [1]

The educational philosophy of Grundtvig is to be found expressed in "Education in Denmark; The Intellectual Basis of a Democratic Commonwealth," which is a symposium of Danish educational ideas and institutions. It is stated as to Grundtvig that he wanted the education of children to be left to

[1] "Bishop Grundtvig and the People's High Schools," E. G. Cooley, Educational Review, December, 1914.

private initiative. One of his axioms was that "Life
and learning were to go together in such a manner
that life was to be first and learning was to follow.
Experience showed that the event preceded the
description, if it was to be of any value."

"He declaimed against the shutting up of children
in scholastic reformatories, attempts at changing
children into wise old men. The early instruction of
children in reading and writing might very well be
left to old women; the education of children was
to be carried on in close connection with practical
life. His assertion that the best boys' schools are
the houses of capable and active citizens, is well
known. He often emphasized the doctrine that 'nothing seems hard to the willing mind,' and he wanted
the children to learn what would be of use to them
in later life.—Besides teaching the practical accom-
plishments: reading, writing, and arithmetic, the
teacher was to tell the children legends and fairy
tales, and the children should be allowed to occupy
part of the time at school with animals and plants
and the affairs of practical life. Instruction was not
to appeal exclusively to the child's intellect but principally to its imagination and emotional nature. The
preparation of lessons was to be supplanted by 'living narrative' (as against the 'dead' cramming of
the grammar school); the teaching of history and
Holy Scripture was to be pursued mostly by the
singing of songs; so Grundtvig devoted his rich gift
for poetry to paraphrasing the Bible, the history

of the world, and the history of Denmark, into 'Chronicle Rhymes' and historical songs to be used in a 'living' form of instruction." [1]

Grundtvig had a lofty conception of the mission of the teacher and of his independence from outside control. He was to be a spiritual leader not alone of the students but of the community as well. His dream was "to make the People's High Schools a center of northern learing—a northern university in the highest sense of the term." They were to be more than this. They were to be the centers out from which a love of country, a belief in equality and a dignity for all classes would issue.

[1] "Education in Denmark," p. 52.

CHAPTER VII

A COÖPERATIVE
COMMONWEALTH

THE coöperative movement is the thing for which Denmark is most widely known. It is the most pervasive thing in the country. It is of the very texture of the average farmer's life. Through the coöperatives he performs for himself almost all of the functions that in other countries are performed by others for him. He assembles his milk and makes and markets his own butter and cheese. He kills his own hogs in his own slaughterhouse and sells them in London through his own export agency. His agents collect his eggs and bring them to his own egg export society where they are candled, graded and made ready for shipment to a foreign market.

He buys food for his cattle in distant lands as well as agricultural machinery, fertilizer and seeds. He manages his own banking, in his own locality and establishes his own credit. Through mutual societies he insures his house and his livestock. He maintains breeding societies of pedigreed hogs, cattle and horses and controls societies as to all of his products.

As a consumer he buys at wholesale and sells to himself at retail. He manufactures many things in his own factory and in coöperation with other Scandinavian countries, he maintains an international wholesale purchasing agency. The Danish farmer is almost as self-contained as was his ancestor who lived completely from his land two centuries ago.

"A typical Danish farm is now connected with the outside world through a network of coöperative agencies. The farmer buys his necessities at his coöperative retail store. He borrows money and places his savings in a coöperative bank; his fertilizers, fodder, seeds, etc., are obtained from coöperative buying and import associations; his cement comes from the coöperative cement factory, and his electricity from a coöperative power plant. He delivers his milk to the coöperative dairy, his pigs to the coöperative slaughterhouse, his eggs to the Danish Coöperative Egg Export Co., and his cattle to the Danish Cattle Export Coöperative. It is usual for a farmer to be a member of at least half a dozen coöperative societies covering the entire range of his economic needs." [1]

The coöperative movement in Denmark is but fifty years old. It had its real beginnings with the farmers rather than with the towns, as in England,

[1] "Coöperative Purchasing of Farm Supplies," by Joseph G. Knapp and John H. Lister, Farm Credit Administration, Washington, D. C., Bulletin No. 1, September, 1935.

and has remained primarily a farmers' movement ever since. It also began as a producers' rather than a consumers' movement, differing again from the movement in England. These differences have continued ever since, although consumers' coöperation has made rapid advances in recent years. It differs again in its wide inclusiveness. There is no country in which it means as many things as in Denmark. It is the very texture of life, not a thing apart. It is the Danes' equivalent for socialism.

Modern Denmark would have been impossible without the coöperative movement. It was the close association and training in the coöperative that gave men confidence and prepared them for politics, as it was the common economic interest of the members that led them to make demands on the government and to send their own members to Parliament. Without the coöperative, the success of the wide-spread distribution of the land would have been impossible. For without the coöperative the small scale farmer would not have been able to market his product and pay for his holding. Nor would the educational system be what it is without this movement, which supports the People's High Schools from which come trained persons to serve as managers and directors.

It is this intimate weaving of coöperation into the life of the people that makes the movement so significant. Hardly anything escapes it. It is the matrix within which the farm life of the country moves. It is a complete environment for the average farmer.

By means of it he becomes producer, distributor, processor and buyer. He is his own manufacturer and salesman. He is his own banker and his own insurer. He borrows from himself and his neighbor and lends to himself and his neighbor. Credit is his servant. It is one of his important tools. And he uses it as he uses other tools. It is almost true that in Denmark every farmer is his own banker, as it is true that every farmer is a merchant. Instead of credit being controlled by a small handful of people, it is controlled by the people themselves who lend their individual credit back and forth to their neighbors to aid them in their undertakings.

A writer in the *Christian Century* says of contemporary Denmark:

"The economic set-up ... is such that it is practically impossible for any one to amass great wealth. This is because the bulk of profits, which go in other countries to the business people are returned to the producers. As economic power always carries with it political power, we find that the farmers and the laborers are the ruling classes of Denmark. These 'common people'—and that includes the vast majority of the Danes—have slowly made up their minds to control the conditions of their living and to make the machinery of life subordinate to the spirit of life; they have slowly learned to do this. A true coöperative society is not gained in a day." [1]

[1] "Coöperative Denmark," by Soren K. Ostergaard, *Christian Century*, December, 1935.

"The wonderful system of coöperation in Danish agriculture," says Harald Faber, "in the highly developed form in which we find it now, embraces almost every branch of agriculture and agricultural industry, and has its ramifications in practically every parish in Denmark. It has built up an organization so complete that all the threads converge to one point from which the joint action of the whole system is in a certain measure controlled. The coöperative movement in Danish agriculture was not started by a circle of philanthropists or even by the landlords for the purpose of benefiting the practical farmers. It has grown up locally and gradually among the peasants in the villages, and takes its root in the feeling of solidarity and a sense of the benefits of mutual help among the peasants which can be traced back to remote centuries." [1]

The farmer is also a local banker. There are 530 coöperative savings banks in the country. In 1933 their deposits amounted to 2,200,000,000 kroner, the number of depositors being about one-half the total population.

The directors of the coöperative banks are usually farmers. They give their services free. They pass upon the loans to their neighbors. Only the president receives a small salary. The banks are opened twice a month for the making of loans and the supervision of the books and the credits. A novel thing about the bank is that the profits do not go back to the

[1] "Coöperation in Danish Agriculture," Faber, p. ix.

shareholders; they are used for educational and community purposes.

As indicative of the stability of coöperative banking and its growth even during the depression, it appears that "the Danish Coöperative Bank had a rapid expansion and 'record turnover' in 1934. Its business more than doubled from 1932 to 1934." [1]

The coöperative movement is wholly voluntary. It receives little subsidy from the state. Nor is it subject to regulation of any kind. The various coöperatives are independent of one another and spring into existence when the farmer finds himself confronted with some activity to be undertaken or some new need to be supplied. The state, however, coöperates with the societies and encourages agriculture in every possible way. Shipping rates on the railroads are very low; so low, in fact, that there is an annual operating deficit. The government subsidizes the mail routes to England, which country is the farmer's best market.

This is about as far as the government goes in its relation to the coöperative movement.

Like America, Denmark has been forced to adopt restrictive measures with regard to her major farm products. Control has been introduced, but a control which has been shared in by both producers and consumers as well as the state. Under the measures directed at economic self-sufficiency it is pro-

[1] "Monthly Labor Review," January, 1936, U. S. Dept. of Labor.

vided that "the number of milch cows will be reduced by 15-20 per cent. Pig breeding will be regulated, and the import of feeding-stuffs such as maize and corn reduced as far as possible by increased production of home feeding stuffs. A rise in the price of agricultural produce in the home market by means of regulation is also proposed and a series of measures are to regulate and reduce agricultural debt by lowering of interest rates and granting a period of respite to farmers in serious difficulties. Restriction on foreign imports of all kinds must also be applied." [1]

The wide-spread agricultural depression which has prevailed throughout the world since 1930 has affected Denmark profoundly, in view of the large export trade of the country. Both England and Germany have imposed restrictive tariff limitations on Danish products. In addition, almost all countries have been working toward a self-contained policy. Along with this there has been a severe fall in prices in the years 1931-32, and to some extent in 1933.

These conditions affected the coöperative movement adversely. Yet the movement has demonstrated its strength by an increased membership and the increased use of the coöperative by its members. While there is a decline in the monetary turn-over within many societies, the figures of the turn-over, especially for production, marketing and purchase,

---

[1] The President of the Royal Agricultural Society of Denmark in an article published by the Agricultural Council.

etc., in most cases show an increase in the volume of the turn-over of goods.

"Now, if with this in mind," says The People's Year Book, published by the Coöperative Wholesale Society of England and Scotland, "one analyzes the figures of recovery, one fact stands out above all others: It is, *that economic recovery has gone furthest, and its benefits have been most widely distributed, precisely in those countries where the Consumers' Coöperative Movement is most powerful* —Sweden, Finland, Norway, Denmark, Great Britain. In these countries industrial production has increased, unemployment has been decidedly reduced, the standard of living has risen. Indeed, so striking is this fact, that in America, where in the first shock of the most tremendous collapse of capitalism which has yet been seen, thinking people began to turn to Soviet Russia for new ideas, and the papers were filled with accounts of the success of the Five-year Plan, this year the center of interest has shifted to Sweden, and politicians and journalists, from the President downwards, are beginning to talk of the value of Consumers' Coöperation." (Italics, the author's.) [1]

[1] The People's Year Book, 1936, article on "Coöperation Overseas in 1934-35," p. 244.

CHAPTER VIII

THE COÖPERATIVE
BALANCE SHEET

A STATISTICAL balance sheet is at best but a balance sheet. Neither membership nor volume of turnover discloses either the working or the power of the coöperative movement. Nor do superiority in values or integrity in dealings. There are unseen gains of greater value than those that are seen.

Some estimate of the extent to which coöperation has invaded those fields which in our country are in capitalistic hands is seen from the following facts:

In 1933 there were 7,916 coöperative societies of all types in the country, of which 5,015 were agricultural, or producers' societies, and 1,824 were consumers' societies. There were 1,077 other types of coöperative societies.[1]

The membership in all these societies was 1,662,-962, out of a total population of 3,550,656. In other words, every average family of four persons was a member of approximately two societies.

[1] Taken from "Monthly Labor Review," January, 1936, U. S. Dept. of Labor.

In addition, there were 329,000 members of consumers' societies representing 9.27% of the total population.

The percentage is much higher among the farmers. In the producers' coöperatives and agricultural purchasing societies, there were 584,016 members, or 39.83% of the total rural population, which numbered 1,466,214.

To this is to be added 749,946 members of other types of coöperatives, representing 21.12% of the total population. This includes membership in credit societies, workers' productive and labor associations, housing and construction societies and other kinds of associations.

From this we see how widely the average person, and especially the average farmer, is identified with the movement. In considering total membership it should be remembered that many people are members of a number of societies. About 200,000 farmers are members of coöperative societies, most of whom are heads of families.

The economic importance of the movement as related to the processing and marketing of farm products will be seen from the following figures for the year 1933: [1]

The Coöperative Dairies dealt with 90% of all the milk supplied by all dairies;

47.1 per cent of the total butter export took place

[1] "Denmark—Agriculture" (The Danish Agricultural Council), 1936, pp. 56-57.

through the Coöperative Butter Export Associations;

84 per cent of all killings in Export Slaughter-houses were done in Coöperative Bacon Factories;

The Danish Coöperative Egg Export and the Co-operative Bacon Factories dealt with 25.1 per cent of the total egg export;

Of the export of meat and cattle, 39.5 per cent were managed by the Coöperative Cattle Export Societies;

67.4 per cent of the total net import of feeding stuffs took place through the Coöperative Societies for the Purchase of Feeding Stuffs;

The Danish Coöperative Fertilizer Society dealt with 36 per cent of the total trade in artificial manures.[1]

When it is considered that these coöperatives are in continuous session; that they involve frequent meetings; that they are carried on by farmers and are watched over and taken part in by the people

[1] The extent (1932) to which the coöperative movement is woven into the life of the average farmer is shown by the following table.

	LOCAL SOCIETIES	MEMBERSHIP	KRONER TURNOVER
Coöperative dairies	1,388	189,000	465,000,000
Coöp. bacon factories...	61	170,000	379,000,000
Egg collecting centers ...	700	45,000	13,500,000
Cattle export societies...	15	14,000	5,000,000
Feeding stuff societies....	1,368	83,000	106,000,000
Coöp. fertilizer societies..	1,412	57,000	15,000,000
Total			983,500,000

Taken from "Denmark 1934," published by The Danish Ministry for Foreign Affairs.

themselves, we get a glimpse of the extent to which the coöperative movement colors and controls the life of the country.

In 1923 an official inquiry was made which showed the part played in agriculture by various coöperatives, with the percentages of agricultural holdings connected with different undertakings and the number of cattle, pigs or poultry involved, as follows:

	Percentage of total number of farms	Percentage of total live stock, etc.
	%	%
Coöperative dairies ...	90	86 (cows)
Coöperative bacon factories	70	75 (pigs)
Local egg-collecting centers	22	26 (poultry)
Cattle export societies.	11	18 (cattle)
Feeding-stuff societies.	31	33 (cows)
Coöp. fertilizer societies	24	29 (area)

These include the major forms of producers' coöperation. Through them upwards of 200,000 farm families perform the functions of entrepreneur for themselves, not through state socialism but through voluntary organizations differing only in motive from the purely private corporation. They themselves produce and sell their butter, cheese and dairy products. They own their own slaughterhouses in the neigh-

borhood of their farms and kill and sell their own
cattle and hogs. They collect their own eggs, grade
them, standardize them and distribute them to the
domestic and foreign market. Through them they
buy their own fertilizer, feed and cement. The farmers function through their local societies, a separate society for each commodity or undertaking,
which are in turn combined in a number of regional
federations, and these again are joined together in
national associations.

According to an article in the *Christian Century*
(December 25, 1935) written by a Dane, the distribution of the consumer's dollar in Denmark is
almost exactly the reverse of its distribution in America. Thus, it is stated that out of the dollar spent
by the consumer for ten foods in the United States
in 1934, 38.5 cents went to the farmer and 61.5 cents
went to the distributors and processors. As compared
with this, it appears from the Danish Statistical
Yearbook (1934) that the consumer's dollar of the
Danes in 1933 was distributed 63.4 cents to the
farmer and 36.6 cents to the distributors and
processors.

Comparisons as to distribution costs in different
countries involve so many different factors and conditions that it is difficult to appraise these factors
with accuracy. Even allowing for a degree of error,
the gains which are enjoyed by the Danish farmer
from being his own processor and distributor are of
vast importance in explaining his high standard of

living and income. But even these gains are secondary to the gains which have come from the independence of the farmer and his control of his industry in all of its relations with the outside world. This, with the improvement in the quality of the product, the adoption of high grades and standards, the pride which the Danish farmer takes in the perfection of his activities, are of greater value than the purely economic savings which are involved.

The societies and activities thus far described in detail relate only to producers coöperatives, to the organized effort of the farmers to protect themselves from middlemen and processors, who otherwise would control their market and determine what the farmer should receive for his produce. Consumers coöperation is of a different sort. The buying and selling of goods for consumers for home consumption is also on a nation-wide scale. Thus, the volume of retail trade, as to those commodities which passed through consumer coöperative channels in 1933, was from 17% to 20% of the total retail trade of the country.

In 1933-34 the sales of 1,815 local consumers' societies amounted to $73,164,000.

Practically all of the consumer societies are affiliated with a wholesale coöperative. The larger one, the famed Danish Distributive Coöperative (wholesale) Society or F. D. B., did a business amounting to $40,709,200 in 1933, and $45,024,000 in 1934. Of this, it produced in 1933 goods to the value of $11,-

497,200, and of $11,504,457 in 1934. The smaller wholesale society or the Ringkobing has 69 affiliated societies and in 1933 did a $830,800 business, and in 1934, a total of $911,200.

Over and above all of the farm coöperatives and the consumer coöperatives is the Union of Danish Coöperative Societies, which looks after the joint interest of the local societies and regional and national associations, furnishing them with information and publishing a coöperative journal.

At the heart of coöperative credit in Denmark is the Danish Coöperative Bank. Its principal office is located in Copenhagen. The capital stock is held by numerous consumers' coöperative societies, coöperative dairies, coöperative food-stuff societies, coöperative savings societies and other coöperative societies and individuals. Membership in the Bank by coöperative societies is increasing steadily. A guarantee capital of about 9,000,000 Kroner was subscribed after favorable action by the Coöperative Congress in 1932.

The combined membership and operation of both producers and consumers coöperatives of all kinds for the years 1900, 1914 and 1933, shown on the following page exhibits the growth of the coöperative movement since the turn of the century.

Consumers coöperation is not confined to the buying and selling of merchandise and farm supplies. The movement has invaded other fields. There are coöperative cement and fertilizer plants and canning

ALL COÖPERATIVE SOCIETIES*
NUMBER OF MEMBERS, SOCIETIES, TURNOVER

	Associations and Societies			Number of Members			Turnover (in Million Kroner)		
	1900	1914	1933 [1]	1900	1914	1933	1900	1914	1933
Societies for Production and Sale									
Coöperative Dairies	1,032	1,168	1,402	140,000	175,000	190,000	135.0	310.0	445.0
Coöperative Butter Export Soc.	3	6	11		268	641	12.7	39.7	134.3
Coöperative Bacon Factories (Slaughter Houses)	26	46	60	60,000	135,000	179,873	35.2	179.4	470.8
Coöperative Egg Export Soc.	370	550	700	25,000	45,000	45,000	2.2	9.3	21.0
Coöperative Seed Supply Soc.	...	1	1	...	1,570	3,400	..	1.5	3.7
Coöperative Cattle Export Soc.	...	8	15	...	5,400	12,227	..	3.9	4.8
Total	1,431	1,779	2,189	225,103	362,238	431,141	185.1	543.8	1,079.6
Societies for Agricultural Supplies (Purchasing)									
Soc. for Purchase of Food Stuffs	110	1,141	1,387	6,250	59,334	89,473	3.7	71.8	90.1
Coöperative Manure Supply	...	763	1,450	...	15,642	60,000	..	5.3	16.1
Dairy Societies' Purchase and Machine Supply	...	1	1	...	961	1,680	..	2.1	6.6
Coöperative Cement Factory	...	1	1	...	837	1,097	..	1.1	3.0
Coöperative Coal Supply	...	1	2	...	465	625	..	1.1	6.8
Total	110	1,907	2,841	6,250	77,239	152,875	3.7	81.4	122.6
Consumer Coöperatives	837	1,562	1,824	130,131	243,855	335,900	38.4	175.8	402.6
Other Coöperatives									
Insurance, etc.	1	3	6	1,115	464,476	749,946		4.2	10.8
Grand Total	2,379	5,251	6,860	362,599	1,147,808	1,669,862	227.2	805.2	1,615.6

* Above table taken from "Denmark—Agriculture," issued by the Danish Agricultural Council, 1936.
[1] Compare above figures with those given by Monthly Labor Revue, January, 1936: All Societies,

factories. Cow and swine improvement and breeding societies are maintained as are seed-testing organizations. Almost every need of the farmer is supplied through one or more organizations of this kind. There are societies for accident insurance, insurance against hail and other storms, and for the insurance of live stock. Coöperative societies exist to prevent tuberculosis in cattle, as well as "control societies" which keep account of the milk of different breeds of cows and employ experts to study the yield per cow and the amount of fodder consumed. There is, in fact, scarcely an activity or an agricultural need that is not represented by its own coöperative organization. Whenever a want arises, the farmers organize for its solution. It is not uncommon for a farmer to be a member of a dozen or more different coöperative societies.

The breeding and rearing of cattle, horses, swine and sheep is promoted by coöperative breeding and control societies. The government subsidizes these societies and aids them in other ways. There are 190 horse-breeding societies, and 1,227 cattle-breeding societies at the present time.

The control societies aim to improve the breed of farm animals by keeping accounting systems as to the quantity of milk produced per cow, its contents in butter fat, as well as the relative cost for maintenance. By such observation the best breeds of cattle are ascertained.

The first control society was established in 1895.

There are 1,712 such societies with 55,438 members, representing 725,351 cows, or over one-third of the total number of cows in the country. These societies receive some subsidy from the state. An inspector visits each farmer within the society every eighteen days. The annual return in milk is much greater in the case of cows under the control of these societies than in the case of cows in general.

CHAPTER IX

HOW THE COÖPERATIVE MOVEMENT CAME TO DENMARK

Up to fifty years ago the Danish farmer worked under conditions very like those of the United States. He was enveloped by middlemen who exploited him on the one hand and the consumer on the other. The farmer had to market through hostile agencies. He had no alternative.

Today the American farmer still produces and sells under these conditions. He produces for an unknown market. He sells to a buyer whose interest it is to buy at the lowest price. This is true as to cattle and hogs. It is true of wheat, corn and of oats. It is true of the dairy farmers, the truck farmers, the egg and poultry raisers and of fruit growers as well. Practically every food product passes through the hands of monopoly buyers whose power is maintained through a close identity with the banks, with the railroads, the terminals, and especially the packing plants of Chicago and the West, and the food exchanges of the city, which control slaughtering, cold storage, warehouse and terminal facilities.

Conditions not dissimilar from these prevailed in Denmark up to about 1880.

The coöperative movement began as a means of self-protection. It came as an economic necessity. Single handed the farmer cannot overcome the commercialized agencies which surround him. He cannot easily organize. He receives inadequate protection from the state. He is at an economic disadvantage in all of his dealings. He often sells at an unknown price and at a price below the cost of production. If he keeps this up long enough he goes into debt. He mortgages his farm. In time, he loses his farm and becomes a tenant. The cut-throat business ultimately destroys the farmer as it destroys his neighbor. This, I think, is true of the farmers as a class in every country where they are not protected from the commercialized forces which envelop them.

Up to the last quarter of the last century, the Danish farmer was like other farmers in this respect. He was being sunk by forces apparently beyond his control. He obtained but little help from the state. Nor was he aided by the large land owners. Relief came by voluntary associations organized by the people themselves. It came through the coöperative movement which had its beginnings a little more than fifty years ago.

This is how the rural movement started in Denmark.

During the winter of 1881-1882, "a young man came to an inn in the western part of Jutland; from there he sent word to the surrounding farms that on a certain afternoon he would give instructions to anybody desiring it on the ways and means of making the best butter. Quite a number of farmers came—and the young man told them how great an advantage it would be if an association could be started, the aim of which should be to engage the services of an expert. This expert was to give instructions in the homes on how to produce fine butter of a uniform quality; he would then receive at some center, conveniently situated for all, the butter which had been churned in the farm houses. There it should be weighed, classified and treated scientifically, welded and packed in butter-barrels. This proposal aroused great interest, for the old ways and means of earning a living (the sale of corn, breeding, and fattening) had no longer been satisfactory, nor sufficient. A group of men arranged another meeting. At this meeting the opinion of the majority was that it would be better to collect the *milk* than the butter. A young dairyman present warmly recommended this, and the greater part of those present approved of the plan to build a common dairy; each man joining in the enterprise was to have his share of the profit in proportion to the weight of the milk delivered by him. The idea was carried out and the plan became reality. Today butter from the Danish coöperative dairies is a well-known article on the world market. Of the sum total of the turn over of butter in the world, Denmark's part has lately been about one-third, and about nine-tenths of this comes from the coöperative dairies." [1]

The members engaged with one another to deliver *all* their milk to the coöperative dairy, except such as was used at home. They bound themselves to be individually responsible for any debts that might be incurred. This made them careful as to the management. For any one of them might become involved for a substantial sum if the enterprise went bankrupt. Any profits made were to be distributed among them in proportion to the amount of milk each farmer delivered.

The experiment was a success. It was noted by other farmers. It freed them from private processors who paid what they chose for milk, butter or cheese and cared little as to its quality. Moreover, the small farmer was helpless, and there are even now 43,900 farmers in Denmark whose farms are less than 8.25 acres in extent. Many thousands owned even smaller farms. They were as welcome in the coöperative as the large farmer. And they were the most helpless in their marketing.

Almost immediately the coöperatives began to improve the quality of the butter which the private processors had not done. They did this for business reasons. Good butter returned a higher price than

[1] "Education in Denmark," p. 16.

poor butter. The quality of Danish butter has since been standardized. It bears a "hallmark" like sterling silver. It is known the world over for its excellence. It was the farmer and not the processor who established this idea. Not only established, but enforced it. A member who does not live up to the standards established is fined or otherwise punished by the coöperative.

Other things followed. The grading up of dairy products awakened the farmers to the possible profits in dairying and to improving the breed of their cattle.

The improvement in the herds due to coöperative dairying has resulted in a rapid increase in the average yield of milk and of the butter fat content. Thus, in 1900, with 5 per cent of the cows under controlled conditions, the average yield of each cow was 6,943 pounds of milk with 3.29 per cent butter fat or 220 pounds. In 1929, 48 per cent of the cows were registered by the milk recording societies and their average yield had increased to 8,217 pounds of milk with 3.86 per cent butter fat, or 317.2 pounds.[1]

How control work has increased milk production is shown by the fact that today the average yield of milk for *all cows* is about 7,275 pounds per cow, the butterfat content averaging some 3.7%.

Cattle-breeding societies were formed. Bad milkers were disposed of and good milkers substituted.

[1] "Coöperative Denmark," by Soren K. Ostergaard, *Christian Century*, December, 1935.

Farmers also took care to deliver their milk in good condition and to see that their neighbors did the same. Economies made their appearance. With all the farmers of the district united in a coöperative a single truck collected the milk from every farm. This reduced the cost of cartage. Other economies were possible. The skimmed milk was taken back to the farm and used for the feeding of hogs. This encouraged the bacon industry which in turn brought about the building of coöperative slaughterhouses. Technical improvements were introduced on the farm and in the dairy which improved both the volume of butter and its quality.

The coöperative dairy spread rapidly all over the country. By 1890 the number had increased to 700. By 1933 the number had grown to 1,402 while their average size has increased.

The universality of coöperative dairying is seen in the fact that of 206,000 Danish farms, about 190,-000, or 90 per cent of all producing farmers, are members, the membership being highest among the small and medium sized farms.

The number of cows kept on the average farm of 70 acres has increased while the yield of milk per cow and the percentage of butter fat realized from the milk has also increased. The number of cows in Denmark in 1882, when the first coöperative was started, was 899,000. By 1914 the number had increased to 1,310,000. In 1933 the number of dairy cows had grown to 1,799,000.

The export of butter showed a similar increase. It grew from an average of 15,630 tons between 1881 and 1885 to an average of 99,420 tons in the years from 1911 to 1915; and from 1925 to 1929 to an average of 141,058 tons. In 1931 it was 172,000 tons. The value of the exports of butter (including cream, milk and cheese) in 1931 amounted to 394,000,000 kroner. 47.1% of the butter exported is handled through the coöperative butter export societies.

The coöperative dairy has been of greatest value to the owners of the small farms, who were the most helpless in their marketing. According to Mr. Faber: "In former times, that is, before 1882, an average peasant farm of about 70 acres would keep normally eight cows. The yield of these was hardly above 380 gallons of milk or 110 lbs. of butter. For this the farmer would get about 5 d. (10 cents) per lb. below the price of 'estate butter.' The coöperative dairies changed all this. The number of cows was increased, and their quality improved. Eleven cows would be the average number on a farm of 70 acres; their milk yield was increased to 550 gallons with 200 lbs. of butter. The quantity of butter produced per farm increased from 880 lbs. to 2,200 lbs., and each pound realized full market price instead of 5 pence below." [1]

Today more than 86 per cent of the milk produced in Denmark is handled by the coöperative dairies while a similar percentage of the cows are entered

[1] Faber, *supra*, p. 45.

in them. The farm owners who remain outside of the coöperative are chiefly the owners of large estates on the smaller islands.

In 1932 the turnover of the dairy coöperative was 465,000,000 kroner, the principal products of the dairies being butter, cream and cheese. The bulk of the butter and cheese is sold through coöperatively owned export societies made up and controlled by the coöperative dairies or by means of direct sales to private exporters. There are eleven coöperative butter exporting societies comprising 621 dairies with an annual turnover of 134,000,000 kroner.

Between 1900 and 1914 the private dairies decreased in number from 511 to 212.

The fact that 90 per cent of the farmers of Denmark are enrolled members of a coöperative dairy indicates their importance to the dairy industry. It also indicates the significance of the coöperative society in the life of the average farmer. To him it is part of his farm. Through it he becomes a manufacturer, a merchant and an exporter. His self-importance and his dignity are correspondingly increased. Even more important he feels that he is an integral part of the larger world; a world not limited by his own country alone but by the world in which he buys his feed and fertilizer and the world in which he sells his product. The psychological effects of this fact are of profound significance.

The coöperative links the farmer with his own country in many ways. It leads him to be interested in the railway and transportation costs. Also in scientific breeding and in the proper packing and distribution of his product. When the dairies are united into federations for export the individual farmer, however small he may be, is provided with as good facilities as is the great estate owners.

By identifying himself with a coöperative dairy the farmer enjoys other benefits. He has an assured market. He is not discriminated against. His milk is honestly tested and weighed. He is paid for his butter fat however rich it may be. He has a regular settlement at short intervals from the dairy which handles his milk. It also makes collections for him. And by means of an export society he saves for himself all of the profits of the middleman, as he keeps the operation costs of the merchandising agency at a minimum. At the end of the year there is a final accounting with a distributive dividend back to the producers determined by the milk furnished by each.

The coöperative is also a training school in democracy. In most dairies the rule of one man one vote prevails no matter how many cows the member may possess. The farmers elect the Board of Directors from their own number and select a dairy manager who is always an expert.

The dairy industry is in fact almost a state-wide monopoly in its operations but a monopoly owned and controlled by 190,000 persons. And it is organized on a state-wide scale. There are 21 central federations of dairies organized for various purposes.

One of these, The Society for Collective Purchase of Danish Creameries, is organized for the purpose of buying dairy equipment, machinery, etc.

As with other coöperative societies the government keeps its hands off. About the only thing the government does is to police the quality of butter. Butter for export may not have more than 16 per cent of water and no other ingredient than common salt may be used as a preservative. The high quality of Danish butter is known the world over.

CHAPTER X

THE FARMER ENTERS THE MEAT PACKING BUSINESS

WE have many coöperative dairies in the United States. Attempts have also been made to establish coöperative slaughter houses but without success. There were too many obstacles to be overcome. They were found in the banks, in the railroads, in the terminals, in unfair competition as to prices and finally in the all but complete refusal of the big packing corporations to deal with any retailer who bought his meats from others than the packing trust. In addition, the meat packers have created the belief that all slaughtering should be done at a half dozen points; points controlled by the monopoly. We have been led to believe that cattle, hogs and sheep must be shipped hundreds of miles before they can be killed and the dressed meat be shipped hundreds of miles back again before it can be eaten. The farmer is forced to sell to what is in effect a single buyer and at a price from which is deducted the cost of transportation which the farmer has in part to pay.

In other words, America has been led to believe

that cattle, hogs and sheep cannot be raised on every farm and killed in a neighboring slaughter house to be consumed in the neighboring town without the payment of excessive transportation and processing costs, but must be passed through a monopolistic bottle-neck, which for more than a generation has been the object of investigation and prosecution by the Federal Government, but without success.

In the last century the farmers of Denmark were in a similar position of helplessness. They were compelled to ship their hogs and cattle to Hamburg and other cities. The market was distant. It was in another country. The farmer had no control over the weighing of his pigs, their grading or their value. He paid arbitrary costs for every service which he received. Efforts were made, as have been made in our own country, to secure fairer treatment but without success.

In 1887 a coöperative bacon factory was established. It was an experiment. The farmers joined together and agreed to be individually responsible for the enterprise and for any debts that it might incur. At the same time they took a new step. They determined to produce a superior quality of bacon in order to capture the English market.

Largely through the energy of a single man, P. Bojsen, owner and principal of a People's High School, 1,200 farmers signed up agreeing to supply about 10,000 pigs annually for a period of 7 years. Stock subscriptions were obtained from 1,100 members which provided a working capital of 170,000 kroner.

As in our own country the coöperative met with opposition. It came from the private buyers. It even came from the farmers. Public authorities placed obstacles in its path. In the end, however, the factory was built and equipped for business.

The experiment met with unexpected success. It led to the organization of other factories. They were established not only in towns, where private slaughter houses did not exist, but in towns where such private enterprises already had a foothold. Today there are 62 coöperative export bacon factories in the country as compared with 23 private enterprises. These 62 coöperative factories slaughter 84 per cent of the bacon for export. Growing out of the coöperative slaughter house similar coöperatives were organized for the export of meat and live cattle and today 39.5 per cent of the export of meat and live cattle is handled by coöperative cattle export associations.

The fact that there are eighty-five slaughter-houses in a country of but three and one-half million people and a total area but twice the size of Massachusetts and one-twentieth the size of Texas, is indicative of the fact that slaughtering is an industry easy of decentralization. As a result it costs the farmer little to bring his hogs and cattle to market. In addition he is able to control his marketing. He is assured of all of the profits and all of the many by-products as well. Nor is an abbatoir the highly costly enterprise it is assumed to be, the average cost of a Danish bacon slaughter house being but $86,000.00.

The slaughter houses are equipped with every modern device. They are clean and sanitary. Butchering is done by trained veterinarians licensed for the purpose. Hogs are killed by electricity.

Pigs are paid for by dead weight. They are classified, payment being made according to classification. This has proved to be of great importance in regard to improving the quality of the product. In addition it provides a uniform nation wide quotation which has been in existence since 1928. The quotation is fixed weekly and is so near the market value that the pig producers practically receive the full value when delivering the pigs. Any surplus earned by the factory is divided among the members at the end of the financial year, according to the number of pigs delivered, after deducting the working expenses, interest on loans, repairs, reserves, etc.

As a further aid to the pig producer in the improvement of his product and especially in its marketing, there is a nation wide collaboration between the various factories. This is obtained through the head office of the bacon factories in Copenhagen.

It is claimed by the private packers in America that only through large scale operations is it possible to save all of the by-products of slaughtering. Yet these things are achieved by the bacon coöperative. By-products are converted into canned commodities.

Edible fats are refined. Pure Danish lard is of high standard and is exported in great quantities to other countries. Hog casings are also of importance in the export trade. Less valuable by-products are treated in destruction plants for the extraction of fats and the manufacture of meat meal and bone meal. A large medicinal industry has been developed.

Danish bacon is maintained at a high standard. It is this standard guaranteed by the coöperative that has given Danish bacon a hall-mark of superiority throughout the world. The word "Danish" is burned on the rind at short intervals. Export may only take place through authorized factories approved by the Ministry of Agriculture. They are subjected to special inspection. Everything which might influence the quality is overseen.

These are some of the "unseen" gains which have come to an industry through other than purely capitalistic motives. The quality of the product has been improved. The market has been expanded. Instead of resistance on the part of processors to proper grades and standards, which block efforts in that direction in this country, the farmer has developed a grading system in his own interest which he enforces even on his associates. The taking of the slaughtering industry out of private hands and its conversion into an industry managed by 179,000 farmers and doing an annual business in 1932 of 387,000,000 kroner is an exhibit of one of the by-products of the coöperative movement which cannot adequately be portrayed in statistics.

At bottom, these farmers are moved by the same motives as private individuals. And the expansion which has taken place is fairly comparable to the best exhibits of American industry.

This is indicated by the increase in the number of pigs in Denmark since the organization of the first coöperative in 1887. It is as follows:

YEAR	No. OF PIGS
1888	771,000
1914	2,497,000
1932	4,826,000
1933	4,390,000

As exhibiting the gains which have come from a high standard of quality and concern for the export market the export of bacon to England has increased as follows:

YEAR	KILOS [1]
1888	45,000,000
1914	147,000,000
1932	384,000,000
1933	280,000,000

Almost every housewife in England and almost every educated child knows that the favorite breakfast dish of the family, bearing the red "Lur" brand, is Danish bacon. It is found in almost every shop. The demand has been created by the ingenuity of

[1] 1 kilo = 2.2046 pounds.

the farmer working democratically through his own organization. He has achieved something which private industry would not achieve. He achieved it by the improvement in the quality of the product and by policing that quality even on himself. And in order that he might control his commodity to the ultimate consumer he established in England his own coöperative marketing agency, "The Danish Bacon Company Limited" which is known everywhere in Great Britain and throughout the Empire. The head office is in London. It handles 30% of the total imports of Danish bacon to England. It has branches all over England and Scotland. It has a fleet of motor trucks which reach retailers in every corner of the country. Its selling organization includes offices, depots, curing factories, etc. The owners of this export agency are a group of twenty-three coöperative bacon factories which also distribute for other factories. Bacon is shipped to England on modern motor ships fitted out with cold storage facilities. In the summer the bacon is conveyed to ports of shipment in refrigerated motor vans from which it is loaded into refrigerated vessels.

As to few food products is monopoly more complete and enveloping of both producer and consumer as meat. And possibly no monopoly is more unjustified or more destructive of diversified agriculture and the kind of farming which prevailed up to fifty years ago. So far as I know, America and England are almost the only large countries, unless it be those of South America, where the slaughtering of cattle is done in private plants. Almost every city in Europe owns its own slaughter house, where all slaughtering is required to be done under official supervision. Many of these abbatoirs are very elaborate. They are clean and sanitary. The stockyards are managed in the interest of the farmer. He can board his cattle, hogs and sheep for an available market at small cost. Slaughtering is done by trained veterinarians, licensed by the state or the municipality. The farmers bring their cattle, hogs or sheep to a nearby city market and local buyers purchase directly from the producer. There is but one middleman between the housewife and the farmer and that is the retail dealer. There is no compulsion on the retailer to buy only from a trust if he would be permitted to remain in business. In consequence, the farmer gets an open price for his product. By reason of the proximity of a slaughterhouse to the farm, there are no substantial transportation costs. Cattle are not shipped halfway across the country to be killed and then shipped back again to the place of their origin to be consumed. Moreover, and this is possibly the most important gain of all, the raising of cattle, hogs and sheep is a part of the economy of every farm. The farmer has a continuous market and a continuous cash income. In consequence there is a diversification of agriculture. It is a year-around business.

CHAPTER XI

THE EGG COÖPERATIVES

THE Danish farmer collects, packs, ships and sells his eggs through coöperative agencies. Most of them go to London. They are recognized for their freshness and evenness of quality and bring high prices. All this is done through a national organization, the Danish Coöperative Egg Export Society, or the D. A. Œ., as the society is called. It is one of the most interesting of the coöperative agencies in the country. It, too, indicates the perseverance of the Danish farmer and the scrupulous care to which he will go to protect himself and the good reputation of his product. The export society now has a total of 700 branches in the country with 45,000 members.

Prior to about 1880 the control of eggs and poultry was in the hands of middlemen who sent buyers about the country who purchased the eggs for shipment to the British market at an agreed upon price. The speculators withheld the eggs for the winter market in order to secure higher prices. The eggs were not always fresh when marketed and the Danish producer suffered in consequence. The farmers tried to control the situation among themselves by agreeing to deliver only fresh eggs. But they were balked in their efforts by the speculators. Finally the farmers realized that they must find some means of getting past the middlemen, just as they had in the case of butter and bacon. So they organized a society to collect, store and distribute eggs themselves. The movement began in a small way as it did in the case of dairying. Each farmer, when joining the society, agreed to subject himself to a fine if he delivered stale eggs. And to insure the date of delivery the society adopted a trademark and also certain numerals which are stamped on the egg and indicate the district and the farmer from which they come.

The export society was formed in 1895. From the start it undertook to be a nation-wide agency. Its branches today are all over the country. Each branch has a distinctive number for identification purposes, while each member has an identification number of his own. These numbers are put on the egg by a rubber stamp. By these means stale eggs can readily be traced back to the seller and a fine imposed. The collection is done by agents to each one of whom a district is assigned. After collection the eggs are shipped to Copenhagen for packing and export.

The speculators opposed the coöperative in every possible way. But as the society sold only fresh eggs, and as it stood behind its guarantee it soon received higher prices for its products than the private dealers could obtain. This forced the private dealers to raise their standards. They, too, had to reject the stale eggs and throw them back on the producers. This drove the independent farmers into the society. And it automatically led to the improvement of the reputation of the Danish egg. In three years' time exports to England increased seven-fold, while the price received increased with the improvement in quality. The egg industry is not yet as exclusively under coöperative control as is the dairy and bacon industry.

The result of the coöperative movement has been to standardize the Danish egg and to raise the price to all of the farmers. In addition, the control of the market by the middlemen has been broken. And just as the coöperative dairies and coöperative slaughterhouses increased the production of butter and bacon, so under the coöperative idea the number of fowls in the country had increased from 5,900,000 in 1893 to 15,100,000 in 1914, and 26,638,000 in 1933.

The 700 branches of the Egg Export Society are firmly united into a single organization. The by-laws require the members to sell all their eggs to the society, to collect the eggs daily from the nests and to deliver them weekly to the local collector. The net surplus of earnings is distributed at the end of the year, one-half going to the local branch for distribution to its members in proportion to the number of eggs delivered, the other half being placed in a reserve as working capital.

The egg export associations had amassed a reserve

fund of $50,000 by 1908 and had returned to its members the guarantee papers on which the original loans were obtained. Their turnover in 1933 amounted to 21,000,000 kroner.

Danish eggs, like Danish butter and bacon, bring fancy prices. They are always fresh, and they have a standardized value in the British market, to which the great bulk of the eggs are shipped. The central warehouse of the society is in Copenhagen. Here the eggs are cleaned, candled and graded for export. Bad eggs are rejected and the good eggs stamped for export.

Bad eggs are charged to the account of the farmer who sends them in. He is warned and fined. If he repeats the offense he may be expelled from the society.

CHAPTER XII

CONSUMERS' COÖPERATION

WE have seen that the coöperative in Denmark is highly developed in several directions whereas in other countries it is often developed in but one. One reason for this is the financial strength of Danish coöperation and its close relationship and sympathy with other branches of the movement. Another is the fact that coöperation has been operating for fifty years in which time men have been trained to think and act together. To this should be added the fact that coöperative banking is both strongly developed and is designed to meet the needs of the man farthest down.

With this background in money and experience and with governmental sympathy for the movement, it is not strange that coöperation should have expanded into so many different fields.

A further factor is the resourcefulness and courage of the people. To channel a pig from the farmyard through all of its stages to a retail dealer in London and to do the same thing for butter and cheese or a few eggs from a farm, but little bigger than a good sized back yard, to the breakfast table in Scotland is an indication that other motives than capitalistic profit can achieve results comparable to those which issue out of purely private enterprise.

While the consumers' coöperative is not as widespread as is the producers' it too has attained a large volume. Measured by volume, from 17 to 20 per cent of those goods consumed in the country, which are handled by coöperatives, are distributed in this way.

The consumers' coöperative movement had its beginning late in the last century. "Reverend Hans Christian Sonne, a pastor in Thisted, Denmark, was interrupted in the midst of a sermon on Christian virtue by a laboring man who said: 'Virtue is well enough in its way but it does not feed one; a piece of bread would be more in our line.' This influenced Sonne to visit England's new coöperatives."

He returned to set up the first successful consumers' coöperative in Denmark. During the next few years the movement grew conservatively until by 1874 there were 92 societies in the country. During the next decade the movement expanded slowly.

About 1885, the constitution of the country was liberalized. The farmers saw in the coöperative store a means of strengthening themselves in opposition to the merchants who were in opposite political parties. From this time on the movement grew rapidly.

The growth and present strength of the consumers' coöperative movement can be seen from the following figures:

Year	No. of Societies	No. of Members	Total Business
1900	837	130,131	38,400,000. kroner
1914	1,562	243,855	175,800,000. "
1933	1,824	335,900	402,600,000. "

These statistics do not include the transactions of the purely farm purchasing or supply coöperatives. The great majority of these coöperatives are still in the rural districts. Of a total of 1,740 societies in 1929, 1,665 were located in rural areas, 70 in the provincial towns and 5 in Copenhagen.

As in the case of the producers' coöperatives, the consumers' societies enlisted a large proportion of their membership from the husmaend or smallholders, 41 per cent (1910) being from this group, 32 per cent coming from the peasant class and 27 per cent from the laboring and artisan class.

One explanation of the growth of the consumers' societies among the farmers is the influence of the Folk High Schools. Leaders came forward from among the students who organized and managed the stores gaining an experience which enabled them to extend its influence over widening fields. This is a major explanation of the slow development in the towns as compared with the country districts.

The Danish coöperative consumer societies, with some local modifications, follow the Rochdale principle in their organization, viz: (1) the sale of goods at the prevailing market prices; (2) buying and selling strictly for cash; (3) dividing the surplus or profits among members in proportion to the volume of their purchases; (4) joint liability of all the members; (5) membership open to everybody; (6) each member one vote; (7) members to control the business through a committee elected at a general meeting of the members, and independent auditors.

In 1933, about one person out of eleven in the country was a member of a consumers' coöperative or one for every 2½ families. This is equivalent to 42 per cent of the Danish households. There are 28,000 members in Copenhagen alone. In 1934 the price in coöperative stores "averaged 7 per cent lower than those for private profit stores and that when dividends on purchases are taken into account the savings effected through coöperative purchasing was 14.4 per cent," according to figures of the Danish Bureau of Statistics.[1]

[1] "Other figures showing the saving effected by making purchases in coöperative instead of private shops have just been published by 'Hovedstadens Brugsforening,' the Coöperative Society in Copenhagen.

"During January and February, 1935, careful check was made on the prices of 41 commodities in general use. The coöperative prices were then compared with the average retail prices in Copenhagen compiled by the public Statistical Department. The figures show that, with three exceptions in January and four in February, the coöperative prices of all commodities were lower than those of the average figures for the whole retail trade. In no instance was the coöperative price higher than the general price.

"The differences in price of several commodities was very marked. . . .

The individual societies found it necessary to protect their members and in 1896 the Coöperative Wholesale Society of Denmark was formed. This gave momentum to the movement. It has branches and warehouses in smaller towns, besides the head offices and warehouses in Copenhagen. The society has erected several factories for roasting coffee, for making chocolate, confectionery, tobacco and cigars. It has a cement, a soap, a mustard and a margarine factory. It owns a chemical works, a spice mill, a hosiery factory, and a factory for men's ready-made clothing. The wholesale society also manufactures bicycles; it imports its own tea; and it owns shares in a shoe factory.

Only coöperative stores can be members of a wholesale society. They organize the wholesale, subscribe for the capital stock and manage the business. In 1916, 1,537 local societies were members of the wholesale, representing 240,000 members. The wholesale society had a turnover in sales of $23,-500,000 with a net surplus of $1,965,000, while the

"Estimates were worked out for a family's expenditure on the 41 items during a year. It was found that a family purchasing these commodities entirely from private traders would, in 12 months, have spent 912.82 Kroner, with the January figures as a basis. The same quantities of the same goods bought at the Coöperative Society would have cost 827.85 kroner—a saving of 10.3 per cent. On the February figures the saving would have been even greater. A year's purchases at the general price level would have amounted to 900.45 kroner; and at the coöperative prices 814.23—a saving of 10.6 per cent."— From "The Link," published by English Coöperative Wholesale Society Press Agency, September 25, 1935.

total turnover of the various factories was nearly $5,000,000. The reserve fund was $1,575,000, and the book value of the buildings $1,400,000.

In 1888 the gross profit was 2½ per cent. In 1921 it was 7½ per cent. The net profit increased in the same proportion, from ¾ of 1 per cent to more than 5 per cent in spite of the higher wages being paid to the employees.[1]

[1] The present position of the consumers' wholesale or F. D. B., as it is commonly known, is shown by the following table, taken from the "People's Year Book, 1936," published by the Coöperative Wholesale Society of England and the Scottish Coöperative Wholesale Society:

STATISTICS Kroner—27 cents	1933	1934
	Mill. Kroner	Mill. Kroner
Total Sales of Retail Societies, which are Members of The Danish Distributive Wholesale	250.0	Not yet known
Total Sales of The Danish Distributive Wholesale	151.9	168.0
Total Sales of Wholesale's Own Productions	42.9	47.5
Number of Societies, Members of Coöperative Joint Committee.......	7,886	......
Number of Retail Societies.........	1,815	......
Number of Societies Members of Coöperative Wholesale	1,833	1,853
Membership of Retail Societies Affiliated with The Danish Distributive Wholesale	307,600	309,100
Employees in Retail Societies.......	......	......
Employees in Wholesale Society....	3,356	3,356

CHAPTER XIII

THE COÖPERATIVES AND THE TRUSTS

LEADERS of the coöperative movement in the Scandinavian countries are realists. They have no hope of any effective control of the trust or monopoly save through direct action. They have no confidence in commissions or in regulatory agencies of any kind. And they have never wasted their efforts in attempting to secure legislation with such ends in view.

From the very beginning the coöperative movement was in a sense a trust-busting adventure. This was true as to butter and cheese. It was even more true as to bacon, and the slaughtering, processing and sale of meat products. The coöperative bacon factory was the first outstanding success in the form of a coöperative yardstick, and this fight against the private meat plants was carried on with so much energy that instead of moving too slowly the progress for a time was too fast. It invited too much opposition from the private traders who sought to kill coöperation in its infancy by paying increased prices to the farmers so as to destroy their loyalty to the coöperative. This was one form of attack adopted by the meat packing industry.

Step by step the farmers have overcome one monopoly after another by mobilizing their own individual resources or buying power in a coöperative corporation and by tenaciously holding to their purpose to make their enterprise a success. Monopoly prices were being charged for farm machinery, for tools, and for feeding stuffs, etc. To defeat this attempt the farmers organized coöperative purchasing societies which have gradually expanded the field of their activities.

In the nineties of the last century the private merchants in Jutland sought to impose monopoly prices on the farmers as to these commodities. This was met by a counter move on the part of the peasants in the formation of a coöperative society to handle these major farm needs. Despite many warnings and much hostility, the society has grown until in 1916 it had 830 local branches, with about 40,000 individual members.

A similar attempt was made by private dealers to charge monopoly prices for fertilizers and manure. In 1915 the dealers sought to force their customers to bind themselves for a period of five or ten years to purchase their entire requirements from a single company. This resulted in the establishment of the Danish Coöperative Manure Supply Society.

The coöperative movement has ventured into

other fields. The Wholesale Society was boycotted by the tobacco merchants, and the coöperative accepted the challenge. It proceeded to manufacture its own tobacco. Branch establishments were later set up for the manufacture of chocolate and soap, margarine, sweets and coffee. There is a chemical plant; also spice mills and a knitting department. The manufacturing enterprises of the coöperatives are growing rapidly.

This militancy of the coöperative movement in the Scandinavian countries is seen in two other courageous undertakings, each directed to making the movement self-contained. The first is of an international character, that of the International Scandinavian Wholesale Coöperative, sometimes spoken of as the Northern Coöperative Union. The central office is in Copenhagen and it purchases and represents the coöperative movement in all the Scandinavian countries.

The primary purpose of the wholesale was to eliminate the middleman between the buyer and seller, and by eliminating his profits to cut down the cost of goods imported into Scandinavian countries. The coöperative makes purchases for the respective accounts of its five national members. It has established offices in London.

From the beginning nearly half of its sales have been in coffee, imported from Brazil, Central America and the Far East. It is in direct touch with large producing and exporting firms in the coffee countries as well as with the European branches of other firms and is therefore in a position to bargain for the most favorable price. The other principal groups of commodities in which it deals are grain and flour, including rice, sago and tapioca, as well as wheat flour, fruits, margarine, oils, bacon and lard, and syrup. Direct contact is maintained with large American flour mills, for the most part on behalf of the Danish Wholesale Society. California, Spain and Bosnia are the important sources from which it imports various fruits, both dried and fresh. Vegetable oils for the manufacture of margarine, largely for the Swedish society, are obtained from European refineries. Coöperators in Scandinavia have long looked forward to a favorable opportunity when they might establish their own coöperative refineries and thus go direct to the producers of raw materials. The sales of the Scandanavian Coöperative Wholesale during 1934 were 32,000,000 kroner.[1]

The second exhibit is an attack on the international monopoly in electrical bulbs. The story is taken from "Sweden: The Middle Way," by Marquis W. Childs:

"Andrews Hedberg, perhaps the leading theorist of Sweden's Coöperative Union, was occupied with the problem of finding some base for establishing, on however modest a scale, a system of production for use, between nations. Aware of the manifold obstacles—customs barriers, national jealousies, the

[1] Sweden: The Middle Way, p. 30.

chaotic state of post-war Europe—he still believed that it should be possible to make a beginning. And the increasing number of essential products that were coming under monopoly control of the great international trusts made it imperative, in his opinion, to find a way to begin.

"The efforts of government to cope with the harmful influences of the trust system have largely proved in vain," he wrote in 1925. "Laws have been passed and prohibitions imposed without any other result being achieved than that the trusts have proceeded along secret lines. Antitrust legislation has, as is realized nowadays in ever-widening circles, certain directly injurious effects from the very fact that it stimulates monopolistic combines to evade even that control which public opinion nevertheless can to some extent exercise if these combines show themselves in the open.

"Meanwhile the Scandinavian Wholesale Society had continued to grow rapidly. But this was merely a wholesale agency, and while it was an important achievement, an important 'first,' Hedberg looked forward to a system of production on the same, or even a broader, international basis.

"To one of the most conspicuous trusts, with price control that was worldwide and iron clad, Hedberg began to give serious thought. This was the cartel that dictated throughout Europe and America the manufacture of electric light bulbs. . . .

"For many months Swedish coöperators, inspired

by Hedberg, considered what they might do. Careful calculation showed that the capital outlay required for a lamp factory was not beyond the reach of Swedish coöperation, amounting to less than the monthly net surplus of the Coöperative Union. But there was one vital question to be answered and that was whether the capital which would be tied up in a coöperative lamp factory might not be used to the greater advantage of consumers in some other way.

"It was true that electrical lamps played a relatively small part in the economy of the average household and therefore it seemed that the potential saving would be small. And yet a reduction of 12 cents in the price of a lamp would mean $1,500,000 saved to the consumers of the 12,000,000 lamps sold each year in Sweden. This looked worth while. And just at this time, in 1928, came an opportunity that was too rare to miss.... The Coöperative Union hired the manager of the Stockholm electric lamp factory, a member of the international lamp monopoly who had resigned, and commissioned him to build a coöperative factory.

"From the first it had been planned that coöperators of all northern countries should present a united front against the cartel. At preliminary conferences representatives of the wholesale societies of Denmark, Finland, Norway and Sweden had agreed to combine forces. Shortly after the plant was completed, delegates from the four countries met again to form the North European Luma Coöperative Society and on May 28, 1931, this international coöperative took over the plan and production was begun.

"It is a true coöperative in every sense, with ownership in the five coöperative wholesale societies. Ultimate authority is vested in a general meeting in which each of the societies has the same voting right. In the interval between annual meetings the management is entrusted to a supervisory council and a board of managers. The council, made up of representatives of the five societies, outlines the duties and supervises the work of the two managers in whom is vested sole legal responsibility.

"The effect on the price of electric bulbs in Scandinavia was startling. Even while the Luma plant was in course of construction, the trust lowered the Swedish price from 37 cents to 27 cents. Soon after the coöperative lamp came on the market the trust had to meet the Luma price of 22 cents. This price allowed for a comfortable margin of surplus—a safe margin, the council felt. . . .

"So remarkable was Luma's success that English coöperators began to discuss the possibility of a similar venture. And promptly the price of light bulbs in England dropped about ten cents. In the first year of its operation the Luma plant turned out nearly 3,000,000 lamps. The 'profit' on this production, with the exception of sufficient bookkeeping reserves, was paid out in dividends to the purchasers of the three million lamps through the five member wholesales." . . .

"Production during the second year, 1934, showed a very satisfactory increase. Total purchase of Luma lamps rose from 1,340,000 kroner in 1933, to 1,810,-000 in 1934. In the second year Luma turned out approximately 3,500,000 lamps, an increase of about 30 per cent. Besides ordinary bulbs for household use Luma now manufactures motor car lamps and a half dozen other special types. During the second year there were no price increases. On the basis of price reductions brought about through the inception of Luma, the coöperatives can claim, and with good reason, a saving to the consuming public of five million kroner a year, realized on the ten million lamps sold annually.

"At the present rate of production Luma is able to satisfy about one-third of the total demand for electric lamps in Sweden. Actually in 1934 the coöperative plant supplied about 22 per cent of Swedish demand. The balance of Sweden's share of the production was exported to the Argentine, Brazil, Iceland, Egypt, and Bulgaria in exchange for goods imported by the Swedish Coöperative Union. And a certain proportion of Luma lamps in Sweden, Norway, Denmark, and Finland are sold to noncoöperative customers." [1]

[1] The story of the coöperative movement in Sweden, by Marquis W. Childs—"Sweden: The Middle Way"—is the most dramatic of all recountals of the coöperative movement. The reception of the book in America is an indication of the widespread interest in the subject, not alone among coöperators but by the general public as well.

CHAPTER XIV

THE LARGER GAINS FROM THE CÖOPERATIVE MOVEMENT

It is to be regretted that coöperation should be so much identified with the country of its birth and the characteristics imposed upon it in that country. For the movement has within it possibilities of fundamental social change.

The beginnings of the coöperative movement are to be found in England in 1844, when a group of weavers organized for the purpose of making savings in their living costs through the collective buying and distribution of goods. And in that country, the movement has remained a kind of reverse capitalism in which the buying and selling of things has been the predominant motive.

Despite the fact that the movement in Great Britain has grown to colossal proportions and today includes thousands of retail stores, great wholesale departments, manufacturing plants, plantations, banking agencies and a combined retail turnover amounting to more than $1,000,000,000 a year, it is still in the eyes of its members, very largely a form of merchandising in which the consumer receives his gains by a share of the savings in the form of patronage dividends.

While the coöperative movement in Denmark has adhered to certain democratic principles written into the constitution of the earliest societies, it has become something far more important. It is in effect a political, social and educational movement almost co-extensive with the state. It is in fact a parallel to socialism, a socialism, however, which exists outside of, rather than as a part of a political state.

Whereas in Italy and Germany the people have lost their personal and political freedom, the reverse is true in Denmark. Instead of a centralization of powers in a few people, there is a distribution of power among all the people. Instead of entrusting the government to dictators the people have retained this power to themselves. In Denmark the state keeps its hands off those things that the individual can do best for himself. Its aid, even to the coöperative, is of a limited sort. Yet far greater gains than those obtained by compulsion have been obtained by the people of Denmark by implements forged for themselves.

By experience, the Dane has learned to work with his fellows. He is good at team play. He has confidence in himself and in his neighbors. He is willing to speculate in small ventures that promise to increase his efficiency. He has learned enough of business to know that he has as good a chance of success as has the average business man. He knows too that success or failure is largely a matter of banking and credit, and knowing this, he has insisted that these agencies should be organized to serve him. He has done the same as to the railroads. Taxation too is studied and its incidence adjusted to those best able to bear. Coöperation is woven into the lives of the people much as is religion. It is not something isolated, as in England or America, it is part of the subconscious life of the nation.

It is more than this. Much as the Protestant religion raised the lower classes to a spiritual dignity, so in Denmark the lowest economic groups have been elevated to a new dignity in their economic, political and social relations. The coöperative movement has reached down to these groups and lifted them into a place of enviable independence.

While not always consciously directed to large, ultimate aims, the coöperative has had a powerful influence on political, social and educational movements, almost co-extensive with the activities of the State in these fields.

It has given birth to cultural values. It has taught the peasant and the worker many things they could not have learned otherwise. It has given them self-confidence. The peasant, seeing a neighbor mastering the details of accounting or observing him succeed as a manager, in turn participates in the management of such affairs and in so doing comes to have confidence in himself and in his class.

Coöperation does much for education. There is a warm regard for art and science and a belief that they are the rightful possessions even of the poor. It has contributed to the organization of Folk High Schools. The State of Massachusetts has many colleges and universities, yet here is a country that is far less wealthy, a country with scarcely any industry, yet it is possessed of sixty-one Folk High Schools and twenty-two agricultural colleges for farmers alone. This is indicative of the willingness of the Danish farmer to spend for things which critics of democracy have insisted would suffer if left to the leveling influence of the people.

Speaking some years ago of the moral gains from coöperation, an observer of Danish institutions said:

"Among the indirect, but equally tangible results of coöperation, I should be inclined to put the development of mind and character among those by whom it is practiced. The peasant or little farmer, who is a member of one or more of these societies, who helps to build up their success and enjoy their benefits, acquires a new outlook. The jealousies and suspicions which are in most countries so common among those who live by the land fall from him. Feeling that he has a voice in the direction of great affairs he acquires an added value and a healthy importance in his own eyes. He knows also that in his degree and according to his output he is on an equal footing with the largest producer and proportionately is doing as well. There is no longer any fear that because he is a little man he will be browbeaten or forced to accept a worse price for what he has to sell than does his rich and powerful neighbor. The skilled minds which direct his business work as zealously for him as for that important neighbor.

"Again, being relieved from all the worry and risk of marketing and sure that whatever he buys from his society, be it seeds or foodstuffs or implements, is the best obtainable at the lowest rate compatible with good quality, he is free to devote himself altogether to the actual business of life. When in any great doubt or difficulty he can rely on the expert advice of his 'control society.' All the science of the country is in fact at the disposal of the humblest worker. The farmer, who, standing alone, can be broken across the knee of tyranny, extortion or competition, if bound up with a hundred others by the bond of common interest is able to mock all of them."[1]

The coöperative movement has drawn the farmer into politics. It has given him a sense of power. And it has led him to organize with his fellows for direct political action. The farmer found that he had to protect his coöperative from the assaults of private traders. He found that the system of taxation discriminated against him. It was necessary that rail-

[1] Denmark and The Danes, Harvey, p. 146.

road rates be adjusted to save him in his export trade.

Mr. Booker Washington attributed the political power of the Danish peasant to the coöperative activities in which he is daily engaged. He says:

"Forty years ago the peasants had all the political rights they now possess, but they did not count for much in political matters. There was then two kinds of butter, 'gentlemen's butter,' which was made on the estates of the big landowners, and peasants' butter. Peasants' butter was worth only one-half as much as the other kind in the market. After the coöperative dairies were established, however, and the price of peasants' butter began to rise the political situation began to change. Year by year the number of coöperative dairies increased and year by year the number of peasant farmers in Parliament increased. In other words, the Danish peasant has become a power in Danish politics because he first became a leader in the industrial development of the country."[1]

The coöperative movement has profoundly changed the economic structure of the country. It has moved into one industrial field after another and taken it over for itself. It has weakened capitalism. In many branches of industry it has driven monopoly out altogether or become its own monopoly. Where it has failed through coöperative ownership it has achieved its ends by other means. It has

[1] The Man Farthest Down, p. 322.

prevented the formation of cartels and monopolies by opening up the domestic market to foreign competition by free trade or low tariffs. It recognized that the protective tariff was a device for the creation of monopoly, and recognizing this fact has kept the tariff so low that monopolies could not exist. Denmark professes to be a free trade country. The average tariff rates have been as low as 5 per cent. Due to the war and the depression they have been increased to an average of 10 per cent.

Coöperation has brought with it specific economic gains. Among them are the following:

1. Tens of thousands of farms average from one-half to a few acres in extent. By means of coöperation it is possible for the owner of a miniature farm to buy and sell as economically as the owner of a large estate.

2. The farmers buy and sell as a group. Acting as a unit they have the power of monopoly, not only of capital but of brains as well. The farmers receive the profits that in other countries go to speculators and middlemen. There are few speculative agencies between the farmer and the consumer.

3. The farmer is relieved of the cost and trouble of marketing his individual produce.

4. Coöperation has contributed greatly to the improvement of farming. Attendance on meetings, discussions, the experts employed by the coöperative societies have brought about better breeds of hogs, cattle, chickens and more intelligent methods of

work. Coöperation has made the farmer proud of his profession. He aims to lead in his community and the coöperative societies afford an opportunity through which his talents are quickly recognized.

5. Coöperation has also aided in freeing the country from those abuses with which we are familiar, such as the excessive costs and power of food trusts, of packers, and of distributors. There are no food rackets in Denmark such as prevail in our large cities which add unconscionably to the costs of food and the burden on the consumer. There are no private bottlenecks through which food must pass as there are no private interests which determine how much food and at what price it will reach the market. The private processor has to face the competition of the coöperative. He has to produce as good a quality as he has to produce at the coöperative price. There is no need for governmental agencies maintained at heavy expense to regulate industry. There is no necessity of such commissions as are found in all of our States and in the Federal Government. Nor are there obstructive court injunctions holding up the activities and orders of these agencies. In Denmark these abuses find a solution through natural processes. They find them through an approach to free trade with the outside world. They find them through the public ownership of the railways. Most important of all they find them through a coöperative society paralleling private industry and operated with a social motive designed to bring about

the largest degree of well-being possible to the majority of the people.

These and other by-products of the coöperative movement, and the self-confidence that has come with these activities, provide the foundations of the economic self-sufficiency and political confidence of the peasant and the working class.

CHAPTER XV

THE PEOPLE'S HIGH
SCHOOLS

NEXT to the coöperative movement the Peoples High Schools are the institutions of Denmark that are most widely known. Many books have been written upon them, and many reports made by commissions and individuals from different countries.

It is not alone because the High Schools are different as schools that they are important, although the methods of study and instruction are in themselves unique. It is the weaving of education into the life-long interest and profit of the farmer population and the creation of implements which are so closely related to the life, the culture and the politics of the country, that is significant. For education in Denmark lies back of the State while the educated man has become the leader. Only in this case the educated man is also the peasant, and the peasant who in other countries might still be a serf much as he was centuries ago.

When one talks about education in Denmark one is talking about something so different from what

the word means to us that it is difficult to portray
one's meaning. The very fundamentals are reversed;
fundamentals which relate to the object of education, the values to be called forth, the way it is to
be used; the rights which inhere in the individual,
and the place of the school and the teacher in the
state. These are but a few of the ways in which
the schools of Denmark differ widely from our
own.

Reference has been made in an earlier chapter to
Bishop Grundtvig and the profound influence of his
agitation on his country and especially on the farmers. And it is with education that his life is most
frequently noted. Out of his teachings the Danish
Folk High School issued, a type of school which has
spread to Norway and Sweden, and which has some
experimental schools on this model in our own country. These people's schools have influenced Denmark profoundly. Without them present-day Denmark would have been impossible. Every institution
bears their imprint, as does the entire peasant population. They are woven into the life, as they are
woven into the democracy, of the country.

Grundtvig never had a school of his own. It was
Kristen Kold that brought the first People's High
School to realization. Kold was by birth a peasant.
In his early youth he had received a scanty educa-
tion. He too revolted against the mechanical
methods of traditional education. Most of all he re-

sented the examinations, tests and catechisms. These protests closed professional opportunity to him and he became a bookbinder. By chance he became acquainted with Grundtvig and in his teachings found more than a justification of his own rebellions. He was inspired to start a personal school where instruction should be through the teacher rather than through the printed page. The school was opened in 1851 at Ryslinge with a few pupils. It grew rapidly until it had a hundred pupils. Women asked to be admitted, so he opened a school for them in the summer, which was the season when men could not be spared from the farm.

Kold, though of peasant origin, was a man of extraordinary ability when it came to understanding the common people and it was through his teaching methods and their justifications by results that the principles of Grundtvig became the accepted principles of all the schools that have since been established.

A Danish treatise on "Education in Denmark" says of Kold: "It was his conviction that a word coming from his inmost soul and understood by the young people could awaken and mold their minds without the use of books or any other instrument. He did not even permit his audience to take notes during the lectures, because that might disturb the spiritual influence." ... "Kold was a true genius as a pedagogue, because his words went straight to the soul of his audience, stirring the inner life of those rather uneducated young people who frequented his school and thus starting them on their quest of that education which later on became so useful to them. When a couple of young farm hands asked him what benefit they could derive from being his pupils, he answered: 'At home we used to have a grandfather's clock which would go for a week when wound up, but I shall wind you up so that never in your life will you stop again ... When I am inspired I can talk so that my audience will remember it even beyond the grave.' ... Outside school he did a great deal of talking individually to the pupils and also at meals when they were all together." He "made the young men realize the vital necessity of 'keeping their feet on the ground.' He taught them that it is quite possible to have a noble mind and yet milk cows or do other manual work at the same time.... Danish produce has become famous abroad and that is due not only to the splendid machinery, but also and chiefly to the wide-awake intelligence and lively interest shown by the young people in its production.... Even if they (the schools) did not take active part in the political movements of the day they strongly influenced the new democracy, giving people the ideas and information necessary in the struggle for self-government." [1]

These schools, with their 6,400 students in annual

[1] Education in Denmark, p. 72.

attendance, from a country but twice the size of Massachusetts, are like the River Nile. They are a continuing freshening influence. They are a more powerful formative influence than the press, than the King, than statesmen. They are the public opinion of the country; a public opinion that is severely honest. It dare not be otherwise. They are a kind of composite conscience demanding integrity in thinking and honest action on the part of the individual, the group or a party.

The schools are not for children. They are for mature boys and girls and for adults. It is part of their philosophy that students should come to them after they have had three or four years of work on the farm. The average age of the pupils is twenty, but many adults from thirty to sixty years attend. The course for men is in the winter and is of five months' duration. The session for women is in the summer and is of three months. As the students are of mature age and as they want to secure the best possible returns for their money, those schools where the teaching is best attract the largest attendance. And because the schools are private and center about the personality of the teacher there is absolute freedom of instruction and discussion. The teacher can say what he pleases. He cannot be interfered with by the state or even by the local trustees. The schools are teachers' schools. The material endowment is secondary. There are no fixed standards of scholarships, no degrees, no tests or examinations of any kind.

The pupils live in or near the school. Board and tuition are very low and deserving students receive assistance from the government upon the recommendation of local committees. The number of students in the schools ranges from ten to four hundred. About three-fourths of the students are middle-class farmers and small holders.

Just as there are no examinations within the schools, so the teachers are not required to pass any official tests. They are appointed by the school principal and are selected for their ability to impart information. They must have personal magnetism and executive ability.

A study of education as related to the coöperative movement was made in 1925 with reference to the needs of India by C. F. Strickland entitled, "Studies In European Coöperation." Interpreting the People's High Schools he said, "The object is not to impart information but to awaken the young adult mind; to teach the young man (or woman) to use his eyes and ears, to understand what he sees and hears, to *wish* to understand and know.... The pupils discuss questions on which a teacher or one of their own number has read a thesis, or hold debates, sometimes in the form of a mimic parliament. The function of the teacher is to evoke, stimulate and guide their thought, not to instill his knowledge into his pupils. . . . He aims rather at equipping them as men and citizens to play an intelligent and patriotic part in their daily life. Hence they examine the administration of their village or county, the constitution of the provincial and national government, and the laws which affect themselves in their normal occupations. Their education has that rural bias and rural atmosphere which so many nations desire, and so few are able to create. The finished pupil neither leaves his country nor his village; he returns to his farm and cultivates the land. . . .

"The passion of enthusiasm and self-sacrifice which animates the teachers in such schools of national citizenship is more easily imagined than reproduced. The sentiment of the pupils is earnest and devoted, of the teachers generous and fraternal; in particular the influence of the head master is potent. . . . Men and women are attracted from all districts and provinces, occasionally also from other countries, by the personality of the head master; they come to 'sit at his feet.'

. . . "The Folk High Schools . . . are often founded and owned by an individual who feels a 'vocation' to the duty of national uplift. . . . The head master is always left as free a control as possible in order that his spiritual influence may not be cramped but may permeate every person and every place."

Speaking of the teachers, the report says, "Their moving force is patriotism, and the feeling of brotherhood guides their work. There are no marks or examinations, though a certificate of attendance is usually given to a pupil at the end of his course. The schools are subject to a periodical state inspection, since they receive a state grant, but it is for the most part left to the nation to estimate their value, and a school which does not inspire will lapse for lack of pupils."...

"The fees of a High School for a winter course will be from 10 kroners to 100 kroners ($2.70 to $27.00).... The fees are received by the schools, not by the Government.... The charge for board and lodging may be 40 or 50 kroners monthly ($10.80 to $13.50). Roughly speaking a pupil may pay 70 or 80 kroners ($18.90 to 21.60) in all per mensum. ... The expenses of the school consist of rent and maintenance of buildings, the pay of teachers, school apparatus and light and fuel...."[1]

The high schools receive some aid from the state in an amount equal to about one-half of the amount of the teachers' salaries. This however is viewed as a kind of indirect grant to provide for pupils who are unable to pay for their own schooling. In 1932-1933, 3,500 students at the high schools and agricultural schools were supported by the state, the state grants to these schools being about 1,300,-000 kroner. The state however exercises no super-

[1] Studies in European Coöperation, by C. F. Strickland, Supt., Government Printing, Punjab, India. Vol. 2, pp. 178-181.

vision over the methods of teaching employed or in the selection of teachers. The schools are private establishments in every sense of the word. They are started by men who feel that they have a message to give, who want to be teachers, who want to enjoy independence of expression and who look to the community for only such help as comes from the use of the school and participation in its extra mural activities. The schools are in effect owned by the principals. They are like our private schools in this respect.

Aside from their influence these schools are of interest in that they involve no tax burden on the community and only a little on the state. Whereas our own county and town schools involve a burden which often equals the costs of all other services and which in many communities can with difficulty be borne, here is a system of collegiate education that is self-supporting. In other words Denmark has created an educational system that is almost as self-reliant as a business enterprise, yet it is so well organized and so well equipped for its uses that it carries itself from the fees of pupils, which for a winter's course range from a few dollars to less than thirty and with food and lodging included do not exceed from $20 to $30.

At the present time there are sixty-one People's High Schools in the country and in the years 1930-31 the schools had 6,317 pupils, of which 3,104 were men and 3,213 were women. As only a small percentage of the pupils attend more than one period it is apparent that a large part of the population has passed through the schools.

Despite considerable variety in the curricula, the schools have common characteristics. All stimulate a love of Denmark and her institutions. The culture of the country is emphasized. History occupies a prominent place. And the study of history is generous enough to include the mythology of the Norsemen as well as the problems of social science of the present day. Singing and literature hold a prominent place, while gymnastics of every kind are indulged in both indoors and out. The monuments which attract the most interest are those of great teachers, of writers, of men of cultural prominence. War and international affairs are practically neglected.

From our point of view the schools are lacking in discipline. Foreign observers remark on the natural relations between teacher and pupil and the absence of rules. The teachers take at least one meal a day with the students, all of whom live in or about the building. This living in common is considered an important feature of the high school idea and may have something to do with the ability of the Danes to work together politically and in their many coöperative societies.

The school day is long and is broken up into periods for lectures, for general assembly, for singing, for periods of reading and study, and for out-of-door play.[1]

In its methods of study the Folk High School corresponds more closely to a seminar of post-graduate students than to anything else we have in America, save that even the post-graduate student is required to face an examination at the end of three or four years, while texts are used along with required reading. The absence of examinations and text books throws the student on to his own resources. He must rely on himself, find his own enthusiasms, decide on his own methods of work and study. Along with this is the daily inspiration from the teacher. There are no forbidden topics as to which the student or the teacher may not venture. The student is assumed to be mature enough to make his own choice while the teacher is seeking

---

[1] The course of study at the Ryslinge Folk High School is as follows:

(School for young men, November-April, 1913)

Subjects	Hours	Subjects	Hours
Danish and composition..	6	Constitutional law and	
Danish History	6	Jurisprudence	1
Farm Accounting	2	Agricultural Economics	1
General History	6	Gymnastics	6
Geography	3	(a) Writing	
Natural Science	4	(a) Bookkeeping	
Danish and other literature	2	Lecture and song each	
Drawing and surveying..	2	evening	
		English, special instruction	

(a) Twenty-four hours in all

for qualities of individuality and for independence of mind rather than the reverse.

When it is considered that these schools are farmers' schools, as close to them as the Grange, as the Farm Bureau of this country and that probably one-third of the farmers or their wives have had some months' contact with this kind of teaching and this sort of inspiration, we have an understanding of the mental characteristics of the Danish peasants, of their courage, self-reliance, and confidence in themselves. This is why the High Schools are of so much significance in the contemporary life and achievements of this country.

The Folk High Schools have strongly influenced other activities. They have created leaders. "The young men, spiritually aroused and nationally educated at the Folk High Schools, became leaders in many respects, each within his own sphere. And this was especially felt in agricultural work in which most of them were employed.... A liberal education, rather than a specialized scientific training, has enabled our farmers to progress in agriculture, in the breeding of cattle, and in the cultivation of turnips, as well as to join in coöperative farming." [1]

"The People's High Schools," says a British observer, "have been described as 'hotbeds' of the coöperative movement; most of the chairmen of committees of coöperative societies, and of the dairy

[1] Education in Denmark, edited by Andreas Boje, Ernst J. Borup, Holger Rutzeback, pp. 87-88.

managers have passed through one or more of them. The high school man, with his love of country and his country's history," says Mr. Thornton, "will take an intelligent interest in public affairs. 30 per cent of the members of the Rigsdag in 1901 had been high school pupils." [1]

Apparently fundamental changes in any country must have a religious quality. The people must be awakened to a passion for some common objective. This is true of Soviet Russia; it is true of Fascist Italy and Nazi Germany. Nations like individuals must be reborn to abandon old traditions and old prejudices. This is what happens with a popular war. Denmark has achieved this emotional awakening by discussion, by education, by rationalization. And it has come through the close identification of so many people with an educational system that they feel is their own, that is devoted to their interests, that owes no obligation to church, party or government and that has consistently taught, for nearly a hundred years, a philosophy of personal dignity, of intellectual independence, of human rights and obligations. Along with this are the material gains that are equally understood by the peasants. The schools have aided in making the coöperative movement strong and self-reliant. They have guided the people to democratic objectives. They have made them familiar with economic changes of value to the majority. This, with the feeling on the part of the

[1] Coöperation in Danish Agriculture, by Faber, p. xviii.

farmers that the schools are their own creation; that they have achieved a distinguished place among educators and that they are an honest expression of the farmers' needs have made them in many ways the outstanding schools of the world.

The Folk High School, though born of a nationalistic motive, has been moved by its principles into wider fields. "A new and wonderful outcome of Grundtvig's High School idea is the International Folk High School at Elsnore started after the war. The principal, Peter Manniche, is friendly to the Grundtvigian ideas on education, but he has transferred the ideas of the ordinary Folk High Schools to a field which is bound to alter the methods of these schools, . . .

"Manniche's chief aim is 'to bring young men and women from different countries together for mutual study and daily intercouse.' It is his hope that the 'International Folk High School' may build a bridge between the nations otherwise ignorant of and perhaps suspicious in their relations with each other. 'The International School,' which at first seemed a mere castle in the air, has proved to be a practical idea. It started in 1921 with 24 pupils from 8 different countries and it has now grown into a well organized school with more than 100 pupils a year." [1]

The outstanding freedom of the principal and the teacher is possibly the real explanation of these

[1] Education in Denmark, p. 86.

schools and their influence. Suppose it were true that in each of our 3,000 counties there was a high school principal who was looked up to as one of the outstanding members of the community, outstanding not alone in scholarship but in ideas and in politics as well. Suppose such a position was sought after by the ablest men who leave the universities and who recognized that their value to the community lay in making the school an instrument of progressive ideas, no matter of what character they might be; suppose, further, that the trustees and the young men and women expected such a teacher to have opinions on what was going on in the world, to be familiar with the experiments being made by other countries, and that if he believed in radical ideas, that he should promote his ideas among them and let them decide for themselves as to whether they were sound. Suppose any nation had a tribune of what he thought was true in every community, who presided over a school which was supported by the community, as it supported a church by gifts, fees or otherwise, and suppose that the school was a continuing thing throughout life, what would be the effect of such an institution on the community and on the nation?

The demand of Grundtvig that the spoken work and not the text book was the important thing, sprang from his recognition of this sort of leadership, if the nation and especially the peasants were to be a free nation and a free people.

This is one of the explanations of the fact that life is such a vital thing to the peasants in Denmark. Life is a right to live in spirit as well as in body. It is a right to use the mind as well as the body. Also that the community and the state are instruments to be shaped and molded by individual wants and needs so that they will yield the largest possible returns to those that compose it.

This, it seems to me, is the outstanding fact of the Folk High School, as this is why the democracy of Denmark is such an outstanding thing in the world today. When one discovers these things in the Danish Folk School, one begins to understand why they have excited men to write books about them, to seek to introduce them into their own country and to believe in education as of such major importance in a properly organized world.

CHAPTER XVI

FARMING AS A FINE ART

In addition to the Peoples High Schools, there are agricultural high schools and schools of household economics which carry the student into the practical field. These are advanced high schools or colleges, and most of them require attendance at the Peoples High Schools as a condition of admission. There are 22 of these agricultural high schools, attended by thousands of students.[1] The student seeking admission must have had some practical training in farming before he may enter, and this is usually received in the years between leaving the elementary schools and entering the Folk High School.

The Agricultural High School maintains close relations with the Peoples High School, teachers often being exchanged between the two. The methods of instruction are similar. The agricultural school is designed to serve the agricultural needs of the neighborhood in which it is located, and usually comes into existence in response to some definite demand.

[1] In 1927-28:—2,230 men and 521 women.

These schools are organized as nearly as possible like a farm. They are experiment stations in advanced farming which familiarize the students with scientific methods, the use of machinery and chemistry, and the advances in the art. Many of the schools are actual farm communities, weaving cultural and mechanical studies into one another in a thoroughly practical way.

A foreigner visiting the high school located at Askov described his experiences as follows:

"Both teachers and pupils are in closest touch with hard reality. They are as far as possible from becoming mere dreamy students. For all around, in rich variety, are spread works of practical utility, carried on by the teachers or by former students, which are quite independent of the school courses, but yet lie open for observation and inquiry from day to day. First comes the Agricultural Experiment Station of forty acres, the largest in Denmark, managed by a staff of six experts and visited every year by 2,000 farmers and others. Here at any given time hundreds of experiments are going on with all sorts of seeds and plants on varying soils (clay, sand, moss).

"Close to the school is the research windmill, built by the State, in which Professor Poul La Cour has learned how to harness the wind and make it generate electricity. And a further walk of 200 or 300 yards brings one to a farm with windmill and power of its own, besides light at will in farmhouse, cowsheds and pigsties. Then there is also the principal's model farm, and a model orchard, showing what kinds of fruit trees thrive best on a sandy soil; a Sloyd school; a school of domestic industries; and one for home weaving. Many of the visitors are cotters, small peasant proprietors, traveling round with help from various funds, in search of practical hints.

"Mr. Schroeder (the principal) himself tells what generally happens at such a visit. After they have seen all they can out of doors, they ask to go in to a lecture, which is flexible enough to allow of a few words for themselves. He calls to their remembrance item by item all they have just seen, and shows how it puts to shame the charges brought from time to time against himself and colleagues, perhaps in the very districts from which his guests have come, of taking up the time of his pupils, with what from the practical point of view is often regarded as 'useless nonsense.' If they had seen so much at Askov on the part of its teachers and former pupils that showed capacity in the practical world, the reason was that the school in putting a new spirit into its pupils and enlarging their outlook— all 'useless nonsense' from the practical point of view —was in an indirect way promoting the disposition and increasing the courage of its pupils, to accomplish some capable work in the world outside. And Mr. Schroeder goes on to add: 'After thirty-six years in the service of the Folkdjohskole, I have not been

able to give up the faith with which I began my
work. Our way through life goes from within out-
wards; if that which is within a man be set in the
right direction it will bear fruit in the whole of his
outer activity; a real enlightenment of spirit in the
man at full age will call forth the energy, capacity
and perseverance, which are more necessary than
acquirements, when we come to the solution of practical problems.' " [1]

The course of study at Lyngby near Copenhagen
is typical of the courses offered in most of the agricultural schools. The entrance requirements include
some familiarity with farm work and attendance at
a folk high school. The school offers a six months'
and a nine months' course for young men. The six
months' course includes chemistry (organic and in-
organic), physics, study of soils, treatment of soils,
including meadow and moorlands, irrigation and
drainage, study of fertilizers, rotation of crops, plant
culture, study of weeds, seed culture, plant diseases,
study of breeds and breeding, judging horses and
cattle, diseases of domestic animals, feeding, horse-
shoeing and smithing, dairying, farm machinery,
farm accounting, drawing, surveying and leveling,
arithmetic, written themes, history of agriculture,
and the study of how to overcome commercial faults
in domestic animals. The nine months' course includes all the above, but is more detailed. Lectures
in sociology and economics, with special reference to

[1] Verdens Gang (Christiania), Sept. 26 and 27, 1898.

rural life, are added. Some work is also offered for students who desire to become "control" assistants, —local agricultural experts offering advice in dairying, fertilization, etc. Those who wish to become members of the large class of government experts in swine culture, dairying, etc., may get their final preparation at Copenhagen in the Royal Veterinary and Agricultural Institute.

The schools described above are for the gaardmaend or well-to-do farmers. In addition there are a number of agricultural schools for farmers having very small holdings. They are called husmaendsskoler, or schools for the husmaend. These combine the most valuable features of the folk high school with those of the agricultural school and make a point of short courses for small holders of any age or preparation. Bee culture, chicken raising and other side lines receive much attention. Any small holder with a problem may go to these schools and obtain the desired assistance.

There are 75,000 Danish farmers who face the difficulty of making a living out of a few acres of land, and their problems are necessarily somewhat different from those of the larger farmers. These husmaendsskoler are doing remarkably good work in helping them.

The Odense Husmaendsskole, which was organized in 1908 by the United Association of Small Holders in the Island of Funen, has special courses for young women, to aid them in their difficult rôle of helpmate on the small farm. There are also two courses for artisans—carpenters, masons, etc.—and two for "control" assistants.

The following is a description of an ordinary day's work in one of the high schools opened in 1865, as given to a group of English visitors in August, 1905. The school described was Vallekilde, one of the largest in Denmark.[1]

" 'The main object of this school,' said the principal, 'is not to impart to our pupils a mass of useful information—that is only a secondary aim. The principal aim is to impart to them a spiritual view of life, so that they may see there is some sense in their existence and some connection in all that happens, in little as in great events. They will thus be prepared to enter on the work of life with good hope and faith, the faith that there is a direction from above in all that happens. The students are of all ages over eighteen years, most of them being twenty and twenty-five, and come from all parts of the country and all classes of society, though the majority belong to the class of small freeholders and cotters, which is so numerous in our country.

" 'Now I should like to give you the picture of a single day here in the winter months, when we have from 190 to 200 young men under our care from the beginning of November to the end of March.

[1] Special Report of the Board of Education of Great Britain on Schools, Public and Private, in the North of Europe.

" 'The bell rings them up at 7 o'clock in the morning. They then dress, make their beds, sweep out their rooms, wash and at 7:30 are ready for a cup of coffee and a bun.

" 'At a quarter to eight the principal has morning prayers with his household; there also are to be found most of the students, though attendance is not compulsory. First a hymn is sung, then are repeated baptismal vows, the Apostles' Creed and the Lord's Prayer. Another short hymn brings the service to a close.

" 'At eight o'clock, four mornings in the week, I give a lecture on geography, and thereby I try to show the audience what relation there is between man and the earth, and how far the people in the various countries have succeeded in reducing the soil to subjection. A song suited to the theme is sung both before and after all lectures. On the two other mornings our Free Kirk clergyman lectures on Church history.

" 'Breakfast comes at 9:15 and consists of a couple of sandwiches and a glass of home-brewed ale.

" 'At half-past nine the artisans go to a special department in a house a few minutes' walk from here, where they are taught what belong to their various trades; carpenters in one room, bricklayers in another, painters in a third, and so on. Most of their time there is taken up in learning to execute working drawings. Likewise the fishermen go to their special department, where they are taught navigation and the natural history of fishes and other water animals, seaplants, etc.

" 'The farm-lads stay here in the central building and are divided into four classes held in various rooms; and for two hours practice writing and drawing. From twelve to one the principal gives a lecture on the history of Denmark, the political history as well as the history of civilization, dwelling more especially on the lives of noted men and women of the last century, whose work we are continuing.

" 'At half-past one comes dinner in the large room below.

" 'At half-past two the artisans and the fishermen go to their own departments again until six o'clock. The farm-lads in the meantime are taught accounts and arithmetic for an hour in two classes. At half-past three these last have gymnastics according to Ling's system.

" 'At five various teachers lecture to the farm-lads only, on physics, on the geography of Denmark, on hygiene, and the history of the world.

" 'At six supper is taken.

" 'From 7:30 to 8:30 lectures for the whole school are given on the history of Danish literature by Mr. Hansen, and on various subjects by the other teachers, Mrs. Hansen twice a week reading aloud from the best of our poets, and I once a week showing lantern slides or glass photographs from all parts of the world, and explaining them to the pupils.

" 'From 8:30 to 9:30 the artisans and fishermen

have their gymnastics while the others have leisure time for the rest of the evening. But you will understand there is not much leisure time for any of them; what there is is used for writing letters, reading, conversing, playing or short walks.

" 'At 10:30 the electric light is put out in the school rooms.' "

The women's course extends over May, June and July; and whilst the lectures are much the same as those for the men, every kind of work done with the needle takes the place of the men's technical classes.

The schools all emphasize practical topics, such as applied surveying, geography, physics, chemistry, biology, sanitation and nature study. All have handiwork and various phases of household economics for young women.

In addition to these schools there are rural schools of household economics in Denmark for women. They are located in the open country or in some rural village. They have a little land, usually 3 to 5 acres for supplies and always a vegetable, fruit and flower garden as part of the school laboratory. The courses are usually six months in length, and the schools are open the entire year. The buildings are equipped with model kitchen, dining-room, living-room, chambers, etc., and the curriculum is as follows: Natural science, chemistry and physics, with special reference to the household; preparation of food, food values; the theory of household economics; household accounting; baking; butchering; curing meats; pickling; cleaning house, washing, ironing, etc.; plain sewing, dressmaking, patching, darning, fine needlework and embroidery; sanitation, including study of human anatomy, laws of health and farmhouse sanitation; garden culture and care of kitchen, fruit and flower garden; preparing vegetables and fruit for keeping and for winter use. Other subjects in these schools are literature, gymnastics, song, rural sociology and reviews in any of the elementary subjects in which the student may be deficient.[1]

The feature of greatest interest in these schools for the husmaend is the short courses for men and women, young and old. These courses are two weeks in length, and begin on the first and third Tuesdays of each month, and continue ten months in the year. It is usually the older people who attend these short courses, and they are kept separate from the younger students in the longer courses. All these schools receive government support.

Each of the short, or two weeks', courses takes up one subject; bee raising, seed growing, chicken raising, fodder, etc., and all are arranged for the most suitable season. The students have free board, free instruction and free traveling both ways, and they may, if necessary, receive assistance to pay for the help needed at home because of their absence.

The Small Holders School in Zealand was founded

[1] Foght, The Folk High School, p. 35.

by a man who had great sympathy for the husmaend. An immediate response came from the small farmers, for they felt the need of such an institution. About five hundred of them offered to contribute 5 kroner each ($1.35) toward the realization of the plan. A Zealand town presented some forty acres to the school. The remainder of the necessary capital was partly subscribed and partly covered by a loan from the Exchequer.

Some of the agricultural schools combine agricultural with practical work, both for those who will till the soil and those who will be country artisans, thus aiming to keep alive both branches of industry necessary to a well balanced rural life. Some, like that at Vallekilde, have the long day grouped about three main lecture periods of 60 minutes each. Lectures on such subjects as "Social Progress in Europe During the Latter Part of the Eighteenth Century" are regularly given before the young farmers, who seem remarkably well acquainted with Adam Smith, Malthus, Carlyle and Voltaire. It is not unusual to have both class periods begin with some rousing folk song.[1]

The work of all these various types of schools is supplemented by rural extension work which began in 1874 with a gathering of country folk at the Askov high school for a series of lectures and discussions. Soon other schools began to hold similar meetings for two-week periods in the autumn. When

[1] Foght, *supra*.

the buildings became inadequate meetings were held
in nearby groves. The themes discussed cover a wide
range of knowledge. At first only the regular folk
high school lectures were included, but gradually
the field was extended until now every phase of
ethics, politics, agriculture and sociology are freely
discussed. These gatherings resemble our own Chau-
tauquas in some respects, but have no admission fee
nor vaudeville attractions.

The community halls and gymnasiums which may
be found in every rural district continue at home
the work that has inspired some of the young people
in the high schools. The state also lends aid to extension education by encouraging traveling courses
in agriculture and household economics.[1]

[1] Foght, p. 38.

CHAPTER XVII

A RURAL CIVILIZATION

DENMARK has done what prophets of a new rural life have hoped for. She was the inspiration of Sir Horace Plunkett and George Russell (A.E.) of Ireland. Life on the farm has been lifted into a new plane. It has been made alluring, to many more alluring than life in the city. Denmark is fast urbanizing the country.

There are obvious reasons why the cultural possibilities of life on the land have been so long neglected. For centuries farming was the business of the peasant and the serf. It was a low order of life. Only rarely was it otherwise! For six hundred years the world has been a city world. It has been made so by the Court, by the Government, most of all by wealth and economic forces. Ambitious rulers beautified their capitals. The rich burghers of Italy and Central Europe vied with the aristocracy in the building of guild halls, merchant palaces, and other evidences of their place and power.

Then came the industrial revolution which still further emphasized the city. It attracted the ambitious, the more capable, the professional man. This commercialization of civilization led to the still further neglect of the country.

Even more powerful than these forces is the age long exploitation of the farmer. It is as old as Greece. It became an organized system under the patrician rule of the Roman Republic, when the Senators and money lenders exacted usury to such an extent that the farm population was driven from the land, which was then divided into great estates, the *latifundia* which the Roman historian Livy says ruined Italy. There has been no interruption of the exploitation from that time to the present. It involved serfdom and slavery. Taine has described the conditions which prevailed in France prior to the Revolution, where the nobles reduced the peasants almost to starvation by taxes, by competitive rents, by *octroi* charges on all that they consumed, by excessive charges for milling their corn, for the making of wine, and in work on the fields and roads. There, as in Russia, it contributed to revolution. Everywhere, with the possible exception of South Germany and parts of the Scandinavian countries, the practice was the same as were the results.

America has not escaped the exploitation of those that cultivate the soil. The implements have been the same, usury, leading to farm foreclosure and tenancy; tenancy leading in turn to poverty. The share cropper is not confined to the south. Nor are the conditions which the south presents. Landlordism is not a local problem. And the costs are much the same in one part of the world as in another. Landlordism in turn leads to further exploitation through usury, the landlord being the money lender or the near-by banker.

It may be that we are on the threshold of a new life on the land; a life that is full of possibilities, with a variety of activities made possible by the contributions of electricity and the telephone, rapid and easy transportation, of aids from the government and the rising power of the farmer in political affairs. Denmark has discovered the possibilities of such a life. She has lifted the farmer out of tenancy into ownership. She has protected him in his credit, in his selling and in his buying. She has ended the age long exploitation by the organized action of the farmers themselves.

It was Bishop Grundtvig who inspired his people to a belief in the possibilities of life on the land. And Denmark has responded to this teaching. She has equipped her farmer with many implements as she has filled his life with many interests. And in fifty years' time the Danish peasant has acquired a sense of dignity in his work. He has a pride in his profession. It is worthy of his best efforts. He has elevated farming into an art. And through the influence of the People's High Schools, the agricultural colleges and the coöperative movement it is the most important thing in the state. The debates of parliament, the discussions in the press, the literature of the country direct their concern to the land and its use as in other countries they direct their concern to banking, to business, to commerce and the needs of the city dweller.

The Danish farmer studies hogs and chickens. He knows how a cow should be fed to produce the most and best butter. He makes and packs his butter, eggs and bacon so that they will please his customer. He insists upon the most careful supervision of his dairy and slaughterhouse in order that the reputation of his product may not suffer from an indifferent producer. He follows up complaints from the foreign market. Commissions study foreign markets. Experts are sent out by the government and the university to aid the farmer and his wife. Stock is bred with the greatest care, while chickens are selected for their quality as egg producers. Soil is studied and the latest agricultural and dairying implements are bought either coöperatively or by groups of men in the same village. Hardly anything is left to chance. The careless and indifferent farmer is not permitted to spoil the reputation of the state. This is the spirit that animates all Denmark.

The government grants a subsidy of several hundred thousand kroner a year to the experiment stations. There are in addition over 100 coöperative experiment stations maintained by the farmers themselves. In this way the breeding of cattle is improved. It is worthy of note that since 1897 the value of agricultural products has been greatly increased, owing largely to the scientific methods which prevail.

Conferences are held during the summer and the winter. The state university and the agricultural schools promote scientific agriculture while lecturers go out from Copenhagen to the most remote villages. As a result of all these activities the farmer is stimulated to a pride in his calling. He is not unlike the scientist working in his laboratory. And he has carried something of the enthusiasm of the scientist to his work. This has created a pride in agriculture and with it a kind of farm culture as real as the culture of the university. The farmer has also become a keen and persistent politician. And he follows politics with the zest of the ward worker. He supports a diversified press. He keeps in touch with the People's High Schools. He has created, in fact, a farm life which is unequaled in the world.

Speaking of the improvement which has come in farming and farm products, as a result of this intensive production, the Hon. Maurice F. Egan, former Ambassador of the United States to Denmark, says:

"Danish butter commands the best price in the English market because its quality is invariable. There is no falling off either in richness or in flavor or quantity in the winter. And so careful are the creameries as to the flavor of the milk that there are certain foodstuffs forbidden to be fed to the cows. The utmost care is used by the Danish farmer to preserve the flavor of their milk. That this is successful is due to team work. The natural competitors of the Danish butter makers in the English market would be the Irish for whom the Right Hon. Sir Horace Plunkett, copying the Danish methods, has been the wisest of guides. Irish grass makes the most exquisitely flavored butter in the market, but the Irish have not caught the art of Danish coöperation, and for some inexplainable reason they do not make butter for export in winter. Not very long ago there was a complaint from England that the quality of Danish butter was falling off. It was treated in Denmark as if the national honor had been attacked and whatever reason of complaint existed was removed at once by the unanimous consent of the nation. It was not a local question but a national one.

"The scientific treatment of the cow is never relaxed for a moment. It has become a habit with the large and the small farmer and his dependents. The cow to him is a milking machine whose power of production is to be approached exactly as if she was of steel and iron. The Danish farmer takes few chances. The unhappy chance he has to take is from the foot and mouth disease against which he and his government use the most drastic measures. In one great farm in Denmark precautions against tuberculosis are carried so far that each cow has her own drinking vessels and every precaution is taken to keep her from infection should there be danger." [1]

[1] Address by Hon. Maurice Francis Egan, Government Printing Office, Senate Document, No. 992, 62nd Congress, 3rd Session.

Cattle are generally stall fed. "Practically all Danish cows are kept in stables for the greater portion of their lives. Many of them are lifelong prisoners. The sheds are built in a large and airy style, and the atmosphere within them is just as pure as the air over the fields. For exercise the animals are taken to be watered once a day. The effect of rain and cold on the yield of milk is known to a nicety. Those fortunate cattle which are placed in the fields in the summer are tied to a stake with a range of but eight yards.

"An inspector from the Scientific Control Association visits the farms once every three weeks. Each cow is examined, its yield of milk, the percentage of butter fat, the amount of fodder consumed, are analyzed and the surplus calculated. It is thus possible for each farmer to know precisely how each cow pays him and further to compare his animals with those of his neighbors. As soon as a cow ceases to pay it is fed up for the butcher." [1]

An immense amount of extension work is going on all of the time. There are lectures and circle work. Excursions are made to Copenhagen and elsewhere, while the coöperative societies have special textbooks for the use of the farmers. The papers and the magazines are universally read, while political and agricultural meetings are being held all the year round.

Growing out of the system of education the aver-

[1] Denmark and the Danes, p. 135.

age farmer is an artisan. He is trained as a blacksmith, weaver, carpenter, and mechanic. Some of the high schools and most of the Husmaend High Schools provide carefully planned courses of study along these lines. This artisanship is of special value to the small holder. It explains the neatness and well kept conditions of the farm house and the outbuildings. But even more important it adds greatly to the wealth of life in rural communities.

Connected with the cultural gains of the People's High Schools is the universality of singing. Songs of the people are heard everywhere. They are known by heart by everybody and they are sung at every gathering as they are sung continuously in every high school.

Athletics hold a similar place in the public life of the people and in the high schools. Group athletics begin with the elementary schools and continue throughout the entire system. The school day at the Folk High School is interrupted by indoor and outdoor gymnastics. They are continued by the older people. There is a favorite pastime for each season of the year. This weaving of singing and athletics, of community meetings of all kinds into the life of the farmer is one of the contributions of the Folk High School.

CHAPTER XVIII

THE MOBILIZATION OF
AGRICULTURE

IT remains to consider the mobilization of agriculture, a mobilization as natural as the mobilization of industry in capitalistic countries. For Denmark exhibits what seems to be a universal rule that when any economic group becomes sufficiently powerful it takes possession of the political agencies of the state along with the economic. One reacts upon the other, as one serves the other. We see this in those countries where the landed aristocracy is the ruling class, as we see it in those countries where capitalism has risen to power.

Danish agriculture has gone through a parallel evolution, an evolution which has resulted in a political, economic and social society reflective of the interests of the farmer as a class. Legislation reflects this as does taxation. The educational agencies are distinctively agrarian. The relations with the outside world have the same motive. Danish agriculture has adopted one after another of the agencies of industry until it is almost a parallel to a nation-wide monopoly or cartel. It operates frankly through an agency for this purpose in the form of The Agricultural Council, which watches over the farmers' interests in a national and international way.

The Agricultural Council is officially described as the crowning point and very keystone of the technical and economic organization of Danish agriculture, its aim and object having been described as follows:

(1) "To further the coöperation of the technical and economical organizations within Danish agriculture to the benefit of agriculture and to undertake such common tasks which do not come within the sphere of the separate organizations but in such a way that the latter are left free to undertake those tasks which fall within their special sphere;

(2) "To be at the disposal of the Government and the Rigsdag on all questions concerning agriculture and to formulate schemes for measures of a practical nature to the benefit of agriculture.

(3) "To represent agriculture abroad, including —in agreement with the Government—to assist in directing and supplying information to the Government Agricultural Advisers abroad and if required to appoint their own represensatives abroad to attend to the agricultural and commercial interests.

(4) "To represent agriculture in relation to other
trades.

(5) "To fight trusts and cartels harmful to the
Community."

The Agricultural Council was formed in 1919. It
is now made up of three principal Danish farm organizations, to-wit: (1) The Union of Danish Co-
operative Societies, (2) the Federated Danish Agricultural Societies, and (3) the Federated Danish
Small Holders Societies. Each of these groups elects
six members, the management of the Council being
in a representative body of seven members.

The Agricultural Council is the voice of all the
agricultural interests of the nation. It speaks and
acts for its 206,000 constituents. It seeks to promote
a market for Danish goods in foreign countries. It
sends its own representatives abroad, it publishes
literature and is a militant agency concerned with
every possible collective interest of the farmer.

One of the declared objectives of the Council is,
"To combat rings and trusts that form a menace to
society." Recognizing the necessity of a free society
as to agriculture, it combats the appearance of any
other kind of society on the part of others. And
instead of attempts at futile regulation by governmental agencies it seeks to destroy monopoly through
competition by the coöperative movement, through
state ownership in some fields, and more particularly through free trade or low tariffs which open

up the markets of Denmark to the competition of the world.

The Agricultural Council, like all other Danish institutions, has a broad base. It is organized back in the extremities through the various local groups which exist. It is aided by hundreds of local organizations of various kinds which discuss the needs of agriculture and ultimately register their opinion with the Council at the top.This decentralization of life is one of the distinctive things of Denmark. It explains the vigor and vitality of all of her institutions. There are 137 local Agricultural societies in the country with a membership of 103,000, the membersip of the local organizations being from 200 to 6,000, with an average of about 800.

These local societies are cultural, political and economic. They hold frequent meetings, with lectures and open discussions. They are concerned with agricultural shows and competitive exhibits of various kinds. Also, with efforts to improve the breed of cattle and of plants. Through these societies pedigreed seed is investigated and purchased in bulk, while consultative advisers go from locality to locality to coöperate with the local groups.

The local Agricultural Societies, as are the cooperative and small holder societies, are further organized into provincial associations, while the provincial associations are organized into a nation-wide federation of Danish Agricultural Societies.

Another of the constituent members of the Agricultural Council is the Danish Small Holders Societies. Small holdings were of minor importance up to the middle of the last century. They began to rise in importance about 1880, with the introduction of the coöperative movement and later with the distribution of the land into peasant holdings. The growth of influence by the small holders societies parallels the rise of the small holder in agriculture and his aggressive participation in the affairs of the state. In 1905 there were 140 such societies with but 9,000 members. By 1915 the number of societies had grown to 887 with 53,600 members, while in 1920 there were 1,102 societies with 81,360 members. At present there are 1,250 societies and 81,300 members.

These local small holders societies, like the agricultural societies, devote themselves to the improvement of local agriculture, to the betterment of their herds, to breeding, poultry keeping, seed culture, and the like. They are also definitely political minded, possibly more frankly political minded than any other class in the nation. Their interests are directed to the general improvement of the Husmaend, to the promotion of peasant proprietorship, to cheap credit, taxation, and to the easy distribution of the land into small holdings.

The political program of the small holders, adopted at a national meeting of delegates in 1913, contained the following demands:

"Equal and general franchise for all men and women of age. Public help in case of need shall deprive no one of his franchise when the distress was not brought about by his own fault.

"The right of the people to the soil of the country to be strengthened and extended.

"The value of the land both in town and country being due to the life and action of the community, the aim shall be by means of a land-tax to take over the values created by the community so as to make them public property. Until this is obtained a tax with an ever increasing rate on property and income shall be maintained.

"In order the more to further the access of the working people to land the Government shall, without loss of interest, offer loans for the erection of small-holdings, to societies for buying up estates for the purpose of subdividing these, to building societies and similar objects. The holdings become freeholds except that interest on the value of the land remains a fixed public tax to the Government.

"Entailed landed properties become free and the increase in value caused thereby shall go to the public exchequer and the interest of the community in these properties shall be safeguarded.

"Financial customs duties shall be gradually reduced until they are totally abolished. Protective duties shall be abolished systematically and gradually.

"The system of education, in schools both for children and youths, shall be so arranged that all have equal admission to a thorough education according to abilities and desire. The right of the homes to regulate the affairs of the school shall be strengthened and extended. Hygiene and abstinence from alcohol to be fixed subjects in the instruction in the schools."

The Government makes a grant of about one million kroner to the general work of the agricultural and small-holders' societies, to cattle shows, breeding societies and other work, but the main part of these expenses is defrayed by members' contributions or other income.

A society of more recent date is the Central Association of Societies of "Twelves", formed in 1923, representing particularly the large landed properties, by the coöperation of the local societies of "Twelves", each of these consisting of from 12 to 14 large farmers or estate owners from a district and dealing with the social and economic interests of the members.

CHAPTER XIX

A FINAL FACTOR IN
DANISH DEMOCRACY

THERE are three recognized claimants in the distribution of wealth. They are labor, capital and land. Labor receives wages, the capitalist receives profit and interest, the landlord receives rent. The coöperative movement is directed to getting rid of private profits; profits taken by the processors and distributors. The mutual and coöperative banks reduce the factor of interest as do the credit facilities provided by the state. There remains the final factor of rent; that is the rent for the use of the land. It remains to be seen how the Danes have minimized the claims of the landlords as they have minimized the claims of the capitalists.

The Scandinavian countries escaped the worst features of the feudal system which for 2,000 years was all but universal in Europe. In Denmark there had always been a substantial number of independent farmers. The majority, however, were but little better than serfs. They held their farms at the will of the landlord and enjoyed practically no civil or political rights. The peasant worked three or four days a week for the estate owner and was paid in grain, hay or a little cash. In effect, he was attached to the large land owner; he was part of his land.

As early as 1800 measures were taken to improve the condition of the peasant. It was forbidden to merge the peasant farms with the larger properties. In 1788 villeinage was abolished, while free-hold ownership was encouraged in a variety of ways. In 1834 the peasants were given some political rights through advisory assemblies. It was not until 1848, however, with the coming of a liberal constitution, that the peasant began to rise. But it was the teachings of Bishop Grundtvig (1783-1872) that lifted the peasant out of his neglected status and awakened him to a belief in the possibility of both political and economic power.

The collapse of Danish agriculture devoted to grain and cattle in the seventies of the last century made the large estate less profitable than it had been, and led the owners to look with favor on a more intensive kind of farming and the distribution of their estates into small holdings.

The last forty years have witnessed a developing program of farm ownership; a program which reflects the opinions and interests of the farm group enjoying political power. The early legislation was largely influenced by the great estate owners. This in turn was modified by the Gaardmaend or middle class farmers, while the present laws on the subject are largely reflective of demands of the small holders or Husmaend. In other words, the land policy is a reflection of the group which controls the parliamentary majority. In this evolution the drift has been continually downward. It involved, first, the control of the lower house of parliament, then the control of the upper house, and, finally, the control of the ministry.

In recent years the present government, composed of Husmaend, agricultural workers and the wage earners of the towns and cities, came into power and secured the enactment of legislation under which the state is now operating.

The first important measure directed to peasant ownership was enacted in 1899. This measure had the approval of the large estate owners who were suffering from the decay of large-scale agriculture and who were agreed that a more intensive type of farming was necessary. This could best be obtained through small holdings. Moreover, many estate owners were willing to permit of the partial division of their estates provided that the tenant and agricultural workers would still work on their lands. With this in view the holdings were limited to approximately five acres while the purchaser negotiated with the land owner as to the price he should pay. Under this arrangement the homesteader was required to provide 10% of the cost of the land, buildings, live stock and other equipment, the government providing the other 90%. In connection with this

program the governmental advance was limited
to 3,600 kroners per farm at 3% interest and was
secured by a first mortgage.

This legislation did not satisfy the tenants or the
Husmaend class. It was obviously in the interest of
the landed aristocracy. Moreover, it left the purchaser still a worker on a large estate obtaining a
supplementary income from his own small holding.
The peasant desired to be completely self-supporting
on his own farm, and during the next ten years legislation was liberalized with the aim of increasing
the size of holdings and of satisfying the demands of
the Husmaend who were rising to political power.
This was done in two ways. The average loan value
was increased to 5,000 kroner with an annual ap-
propriation by parliament of 3,000,000 kroner to aid
in the purchase. The provisions of the law were
extended to include others than agricultural workers.
It was made possible for garden and nursery workers,
brickmakers, tinkers, etc., to enjoy the provisions
of the Act. A further liberalization of the law was
provided in 1909 by an increase in the annual appro-
priation to 4,000,000 kroner, while the maximum
loan to purchasers was raised to 6,500 kroner.

Two general policies have been followed. Under
the early program the settler obtained his holding
in the open market from an existing land owner. In
making the purchase he was aided by the state
through a permanent committee or through the Commission on Small Holdings. The state concerned it-

self to see that the land was bought at the proper price and that the holding acquired offered a reasonable security for the loan by the state to the settler.

In order to secure this aid the applicant was required to be a citizen, usually between 25 and 50 years of age. He must be of good character and not have received parish relief, which had not been remitted or repaid. He was required to be familiar with farming and to have supported himself by farm work at least four years after his seventeenth birthday. Testimonials were required from the parish council and from two reliable persons acquainted with the applicant who certified as to his industry, sobriety, thrift, honesty, and ability to manage a small holding. The applicant was further required to submit proof that he possessed the means required by law for acquiring possession of the property and that he was unable from his own resources to purchase a property of the nature described in the laws.

The financing involved a government loan amounting to nine-tenths of the value of the land and buildings but not more than the maximum amount provided by the law; 10 per cent of the cost of the land and building had to be paid by the applicant. In other words, the settler was required to grubstake himself by a substantial down payment.[1]

[1] The rate of interest was 4 per cent and payments were made as follows: During the first five years only interest on the capital was required. Then the total loan was divided into two parts. Three-fifths was converted into what may be called public stock and placed on the market for sale with the

With the coming of the Husmaend and agricultural worker to power radical changes were made in the homesteading policies; changes directed to making it easier for the land to be acquired.

Under the influence of this group and the legislation of 1919, and amendments, the government itself acquired the land to be then leased to the occupier on a ground rental lease. Instead of the homesteader buying directly from land owners and often paying speculative prices for his purchase, the government acquired a large holding of desirable land, subdivided it and leased it to homesteaders at a fixed annual rental subject to periodic revaluation. In other words, the government entered into the landlord's shoes. But with this difference. The government fixed the rent at the cost of the land, reserving to itself any increase which might come to its value in the future. The occupier was now secure in his holdings while he and the community reaped the increment which had previously gone to the land owner.

With this as a base, the government loaned the homesteader sufficient money to put up the necessary buildings at a rate of interest fixed by what the

guaranty of the state behind it. It was sold through the Mortgage Bank of Denmark. On the other two-fifths of the loan, not sold as public stock, the borrowing farmer had to pay 5 per cent interest, one per cent of which was used for a sinking fund for the repayment of the principal. When the two-fifths section had been paid off in an estimated period of 46½ years, the three-fifths section was converted into public stock to be paid off in the same manner, the entire loan being repaid in 98 years.

government itself had to pay. The land for this purpose was to come from public lands, from large hereditary estates held in trust, and from the purchase of land in the open market at reasonable prices. The radicals had hoped for more than this. They sought the right to expropriate private estates. This provision, however, had been eliminated from the proposal. It checked the widest extension of the system as it tended to increase the cost of proceedings and the cost of the land.

Under the later Act of 1919 the homesteader does not acquire the land, he pays $4\frac{1}{2}$ per cent annually on its fixed value to the government, the valuation being revised following every tax re-assessment. The government lends the homesteader up to 90% of the cost of the improvements only, with a maximum fixed annually on the basis of the latest price index. The interest on the governmental advance for improvements is $4\frac{1}{2}\%$, and the loan is repaid by annual installments of 1% of the total loan plus interest. No amortization payments on the capital are required during the first five years. The settler is still required to provide 10% of the building and equipment cost. The two methods described are operative side by side.

The post-war depression led to increased demand for available land, and a further development of the homesteading policy was undertaken with the aim of relieving unemployment. In 1921 a law was enacted which increased the maximum loan obtainable to

$6,300 (23,000 kroner). Of this sum the government advanced up to nine-tenths, of which three-tenths was a direct grant, while six-tenths was in the form of a loan. In other words, the government granted a subsidy up to one-third of the amount of the advance. In 1924, the grant was replaced by a non-interest bearing loan to be paid back according to the provisions of the Act of 1919.

Along with the conversion of the agricultural worker and tenant into an owner, laws have been passed looking to the stability of agriculture. No farm can be closed down without the approval of the Minister of Agriculture, and the size of holdings cannot be less than 3 hectares (7½ acres) of medium quality land, unless the Minister agrees otherwise. Since 1925 all farms must be maintained as independent properties with the necessary buildings and be cultivated by the occupier. No part of the land can be joined to another farm unless the State agrees. The area which is considered sufficient for a family is 17.3 acres, if the land is of the best quality, or 34.6 acres if it is of the poorer quality. Regulations and supervision aim to insure a farm which will provide complete subsistence.

Up to May, 1933, more than 20,000 holdings had been established under the Small Holdings Act, of which three-fourths were under the 1899 Act and one-fourth under the 1919 Act. More recently, more than one-half of the holdings have been established under the later act. Furthermore, up to that time more than 11,500 supplementary loans were made to enlarge small holdings which were too small to fully support a family.

From 1900 to 1932 under the various Small Holdings Acts, the state loans and grants to the farmers amounted to 163,600,000 kroner. During the period from 1920 to 1929 land in value of 36,700,000 kroner had been disposed of and 56,300,000 kroner had been granted in the form of building loans. Funds for land settlements are obtained by the state by borrowing. The following statistics indicate the growth of the homesteading movement from 1900 to 1924, with the number of new holdings established, the total loans made in aid of such holdings and the average loan per holding:

Years	No. of Holdings	Total Loans New Units		Average Loan Per Holding	
1900-05	1,859	6,530,233	kroner	3,513	kroner
1905-10	3,233	14,818,456	"	4,584	"
1910-15	2,543	15,717,872	"	6,181	"
1915-18	1,254	9,523,764	"	7,595	"
1918-24	2,562	39,806,678	"	not reported	

Grand
Total 11,451 86,397,003 Kroner
Supplementary
   loans 13,681,919 "

100,078,922 Kroner

One significant fact of the above table is the increase in the annual homesteads provided which has taken place since the war as a result of the encouragement given to homesteaders by recent legislation. A second fact is the increase in the total appropriations made by the government for this purpose. It is also of interest that during the first five-year period the size of the holdings averaged 7.9 acres, rising to 9.1 acres in 1905-10. In the period 1921-22 the average size of the holding was 18 acres and in 1922-23, 19.3 acres.

It is not to be assumed that this program escaped criticism. It was urged that the government was inviting losses by virtue of the financial risks taken. This criticism, however, has proven unfounded. In the twenty-five years preceding 1924 the total loss to the government from the failure of homesteaders to meet their payments was $9,085, equivalent to 35 cents per $1,000 invested.

In connection with the development of farm homesteads, the administration is highly decentralized. The Acts are administered through local county commissions of three persons, one selected by the Minister of Agriculture, the other two being chosen locally. This committee examines the qualifications of the applicant and administers the distribution of funds.

I visited one of the development projects on the west coast of Denmark which is typical of others. The cost of the individual holding was about $6,000.

Houses were of six rooms, with a large detached barn. They were built of brick, covered with white cement. The style of house was that of the average Danish peasant. In addition to the homestead the farmer was provided with 6 cows, 21 pigs, 2 horses and 240 chickens. The houses were well furnished and the farmers apparently contented. The net annual income of the farmer after all payments was said to be about $400.

As in Ireland, the state uses its credit to underwrite the purchase and provide cheap credit, while the local committees administer the projects. This decentralization of responsibility is essential to its success. It relates the buyer to the community in which he settles; it gives him the aid of his new neighbors. It also provides an administrative group familiar with local conditions,—the kind of crops that should be planted, the type of cattle and hogs that should be raised, and along with these things a continued supervision of the new settler.

In this conversion of the farmer into an owner we have the economic foundations of the democracy of Denmark; a democracy like that of France in its permanence but better than that of France in its social quality. Within this system, too, we have the elements of the coöperative movement and a system of education that create a rural civilization unlike anything to be found elsewhere in the world. It is a civilization in which the peasant does his thinking for himself. He decides as to what is in his interest and having so decided he puts it into execution. He sends one of his fellows to the Rigsdag. And he treats the government quite frankly as something that should reflect his own interests.

CHAPTER XX

THE PASSING OF
LANDLORDISM

In the preceding chapter, we described the progressive steps taken by the nation to make an end of farm tenancy by the division of the land into small holdings. It remains to consider the effects of these changes on the life of the people, changes almost if not quite as important as those which issue out of the coöperative movement.

In the middle of the last century, 42 per cent of the farmers were tenants, while 58 per cent were free-hold owners. Today farm tenancy is in effect at an end. The number of farm tenants is in the neighborhood of six per cent according to the last official tables, but this percentage has been materially reduced since 1919 which is the date of the last survey.

The progressive change from tenancy to ownership is indicated by the following table:

	Tenants	Freehold Ownership
1850	42.5%	57.5%
1860	30.8%	69.2%
1885	14.5%	85.5%
1905	10.1%	89.9%
1919	5.7%	94.3%

The total number of farms in the country in 1929 was 205,971. Divided according to size they are as follows:

Size	No. of Holdings 1929
1.36 to 8.15 acres	38,590
8.15 to 24.71 "	71,943
24.71 to 37.07 "	26,852
37.07 to 74.13 "	43,635
74.13 to 148.26 "	20,450
148.26 to 296.52 "	3,428
296.52 to 593.04 "	767
593.04 acres and more	306
Total	205,971

By reference to the preceding table we get a picture of the relationship of the people to the land, as well as of the approach to an equalization of opportunity through the wide-spread distribution of farm holdings. Within this table is a further exhibit of the permanent foundations of the life of Denmark.

From this it appears that:

There remain only 306 estates of 593.4 acres and over.

There are 767 estates between 296 and 593.04 acres.

All save 1,073 of the 205,971 farms in the country are of less than 300 acres.

The large holdings are survivals of the estates of the landed nobility. They are survivals of feudalism. Their owners have lost the political power they once possessed. Their estates are slowly being taken from them to be divided up into small holdings. Those that remain are worked by hired labor, which because of the ease with which peasants can secure land is difficult to obtain. This in turn affects agricultural wages. For the farm worker has an alternative. In consequence he is independent-minded; independent in his thinking and in his political activities as well.

Below these large estates are 90,937 farms belonging to the peasants proper. They range in size from 24.71 acres to 296.52 acres. These farmers are known as Gaardmaend. They are well educated and devote a lot of time to politics and the coöperative undertakings with which they are associated. They know about the most technical agriculture and provide the managers and directors of the coöperative societies. They are saturated with the art of farming as a science and are not greatly concerned with an ambition to be rich and acquire more land. They enjoy a higher political and social status than that of any other farmers in Europe, if not in the world, as they enjoy a relatively high economic well being.

At the bottom of the peasant group are the Husmaend, of whom there are approximately 110,000, with holdings of less than 24.71 acres. Of these 38,590 are less than 8.15 acres in size. Even members of this class make a decent living for their family. They are able to do this largely by the aid of the coöperative undertakings which handle their output the same as that of the larger peasants.

Within these three economic groups are to be found the divergent economic interests which led their members to organize into political parties. Within this conflict of interests is to be found the political and social evolution of the last century. And the political history of Denmark is the history of the rise of the peasant to power and with it a shift of that power from one group to the other. With the introduction of the parliamentary system in 1848 the middle-class peasants acquired representation in parliament. The next fifty years saw this group rising to power. It made its way first in the lower house and later in the upper. It was in conflict with the large land owners on the one hand and the commercial classes of the cities on the other. In 1901 the peasants were in control of parliament and took over the government through the ministry. It was during this period that the coöperative movement made its great headway as did the development of small holdings.

The final step in the political evolution is the rise of the Husmaend to power. They, too, had economic interests; interests that could only be protected and promoted by the state. They joined hands with the agricultural workers and the artisans of the cities as the Social Democratic Party and during the present century obtained control of both houses of Parliament with a ministry of their own reflective of their economic demands. Within the platform of this group is a suggestion of a socialized state in which the processing and distribution of agricultural products and consumers' goods will be in the hands of cooperative societies. Along with this is the universalization of farm ownership and the opening up of the land to the artisan class of the city. To this should be added, and this has already been achieved, a comprehensive system of social insurance, relief and protection of labor in its relations with capital.

Unlike Russia, the socialization of the land is to be brought about through taxation, by means of a tax levied wholly on the value of the land exclusive of the improvements. This with an approach to complete freedom of trade with the outside world form the immediate major demands of the Social Democratic Party.

Within these farm groups and their struggles for political power we have a key to Danish history for the last 100 years. The history is a story of the weakening of the power of the upper class by the peasants and the subsequent weakening of the peasants by the husmaend.

Not only is the wide-spread distribution of land an explanation of the political democracy which prevails, it explains other things as well. The character of education is profoundly influenced by the system of land tenure, while the coöperative movement would have been difficult among any other people than a nation of home owners. Back of the courage, self-reliance and independence of the Danish farmer is the fact that he owns his own farm. He works for himself. And working for himself, he has created institutions which reflect the democracy inherent in the ownership of his own home, his own tools, and his own independent place in the State.

Nor would the People's High Schools and the educational system of the country have been possible had the farmers been tenants. Wherever tenancy prevails, there we have an indifference to education. It is the home-owning farmer who wants education for himself. He wants it for his children. And in Denmark the peasant has insisted that his schools should be free from any other control than that which he himself imposes upon them.

One of the surprising exhibits of the openmindedness of the small owners is the interest found in Denmark in the writings of Henry George. His books have been translated and widely circulated. There is a magazine devoted to his philosophy which has a large circulation, while a political party has been organized whose platform is directed to the taxation of land values, or the single tax.

One would not expect a social philosophy which looked to the taxation of land values as a sole source of revenue to have a following among small-sized farmers, jealous of their land and instinctively inclined to shift the burden of taxation onto other shoulders. The explanation is to be found in the hunger of the farm workers to obtain a piece of land of their own and to obtain it at a reasonable price. The Danish husmaend adopted this program as a means of accelerating the break-up of the large estates and of stimulating their easy purchase by the Government for distribution to small holders.

There is a further justification of this philosophy. The income tax is relied on for both local and national revenues. It is arbitrarily assessed on a sliding scale, a high rate being imposed on land that is intensively cultivated, with a lower rate on the farms of the middle class peasants and a still lower rate on the land of the large land holders. In other words, it is assumed that the small holder produces more wealth per acre than does the owner of a large estate. The husmaend, however, rejects this principle of taxation on the ground that the tax is a tax on effort rather than on opportunity. All owners of land, they say, should be taxed on the opportunity they enjoy to produce wealth rather than on the use they make of that opportunity. In other words, the system of taxation which prevails encourages a dog-in-the-manger policy which results in a lower production of wealth rather than a higher.

In place of this system, the husmaend demand that all land owners shall be taxed on their land at the same rate and be forced by such taxation to either use their land to its fullest or to pay for the privilege of withholding it from its most efficient use.

This movement for the taxation of land values is a further expression of the individualism of the Danish peasant, of his self-reliance, of his belief in the free play of competition, and the resourcefulness of the individual. It is also an exhibit of his distrust of regimentation by the State and a belief that the individual should be aided by natural laws to achieve his own security in his own way.

CHAPTER XXI

GOVERNMENT FROM THE BOTTOM

It remains to consider the final factor in an understanding of Denmark and that is the political state. I have placed this last rather than first because the political institutions of Denmark are a result rather than a cause. They are a product of economic conditions. They are what they are because of the widespread ownership of the land, along with the educational, coöperative and other agencies, which have trained the people in the use of government for definite social and economic ends.

And first as to the framework of government, that is, the Constitution, through which the people act.

My first actual contact with a freely moving democratic state was in the Irish Free State in the summer of 1935 where I saw a government work as it seems to me a democratic government should work.

The Free State is almost exactly the same political age as was America at the time when we adopted our Constitution. Like America, the Free State had

187

gone through a war of liberation with England; a war which not only exhausted the state but involved the loss of many of its outstanding men as well. As in America, the revolution was followed by party conflicts, very like those between the Federalists and Republicans, like those between Hamilton and Jefferson.

Like our own government, that of the Irish Free State was modeled on that of England. There was a parliament consisting of two houses, elected by popular suffrage. But here the similarity ends. In the Free State there is a responsible ministry selected by the majority political party. There is a president, also responsible to parliament. The courts are merely civil agencies for the adjudication of civil and criminal matters. They exercise no legislative or political power.

Even more important, is the difference in attitude toward the Constitution. For one hundred and fifty years we have clung tenaciously to the letter of our institutions no matter how badly they worked or how costly they were. We will not permit these institutions to be altered even though they were designed for a mere string of people along the Atlantic Seaboard and were determined upon when we were wholly inexperienced in the art of government. The Irish Free State is free from such reverences. Like England, the Constitution is little more than an exalted statute. It is an accepted rule of procedure for carrying on business in the most efficient way.

It commands no further reverence from the people or from parliament. If it fails to work well it can be changed, as in Great Britain, by the government that happens to be in power. And it is being changed in this way. The present government was having its legislative program on which it had come into power obstructed by the upper house of parliament. So the ministry secured the passage of a law by which even though the upper house refused to approve of a bill, the bill should become a law after a certain period of time, if the lower house insisted upon it. Even with this check on the upper chamber there was conflict; a conflict which seemed to the ministry to be inconsistent with democratic procedure and the popular will. So in the spring of 1936, a second law was passed which abolished the Upper House altogether. It declared it to be unnecessary. The only legislative agency deemed necessary was a single chamber coming directly from the people and directed by the people to carry into effect a program which had been submitted to them at an election by one of the two major parties.

In other words, the Irish Free State moves as freely and directly as does an individual or a private corporation with us. It changes its constitution by the action of parliament just as it passes any other legislative act. From this decision there is no appeal to the courts, the only appeal being to the people at the next election when the issue may be raised by the opposition party and if the people so direct the constitution may be changed again.

The Danes are like the Irish in this respect. They, too, look upon the constitution as an implement to be used as they would use any other implement. So long as the constitution provides for a way of doing things it is to be observed. But it may be changed just as soon as public opinion thinks such a change should be made. In other words, the Constitution is something to enable the popular will to register itself and when so registered to set it into immediate motion. The only reverence which attaches to the Constitution is a reverence for something that is fundamentally right and useful. Like the Irish, the Danes have been changing their form of government for one hundred years. They have been doing it by discussion. And with each change there has been an advance in progressive legislation; an advance which has resulted in no disasters even to those who opposed the change.

The changes which have taken place in the political life of Denmark are a reflection of the change in the economic life of the country. The political state in fact is a mirror of the economic life.

All this has come about by consent, by debate and discussion. Up until the middle of the seventeenth century Denmark was a type of feudal oligarchy in which "the nobility had seized most of the power at the expense of the Crown and other classes of society."

About 1760 this system gave way to a government like that of Louis XIV in France, under which the king was supreme.

This type of monarchy continued into the early part of the nineteenth century.

As a result of the French Revolution the constitution was liberalized, first in 1830 and again in 1849. Under these changes the country obtained a freer Constitution.

All these changes took place without violence or bloodshed.

Again reaction set in about 1865 when the wealthy classes took control of parliament and especially of the upper chamber. From this time on however the drift has been in the opposite direction. First the well-to-do peasants obtained control of the lower house, the upper house being still dominated by the landed aristocracy and the business men from the cities.

In 1901 the peasants obtained a majority in the upper chamber and with this victory, a responsible government was established with the ministry representative of the well-to-do farmers.

During the World War the Constitution was changed again, accompanied by the rise of a new political group representing extreme left wing political opinion. This group is made up of the Husmaend, of whom there are more than 100,000 in the country, who joined with the agricultural workers and the artisans of the towns and cities. They formed local political organizations. They established their own high schools. They, too, had economic needs, needs which differentiated them from the middle-class farmers, as the needs of the latter differentiated them from the landed aristocracy.

Out of this group came leaders, men who had been trained in local affairs and in the coöperative movement. They developed a political philosophy of their own. The platform of the party is to be found in another chapter. It relates primarily to easy access to the land, to the methods for financing purchases, and especially to the taxation of land values by uniform rule which will force the large estate owners to dispose of their estates.

This party grew in numbers until it in turn took the government away from the middle-class farmers and formed a ministry reflective of its economic interests. It is now in control of the government.

In this evolution Denmark has carried democracy to extreme limits. In the first place, the proportional representation system prevails. Members of both houses of parliament are elected from lists in large districts, as a result of which representation is almost an exact reflection of the aggregate vote of all parties, even minority groups having a numerical representation equivalent to their voting strength. The ministry is appointed from the majority party. It formulates a program and carries it into legislation. Thus, when the Social-Democratic Party came into power it had a mandate from the people to carry its program into effect.

The political parties of Denmark are quite frankly reflective of the demands of the various economic groups. They are like France in this respect. There are seven such parties in the country, each with an economic program of its own. Of these, one is Conservative, with 27 members in the lower house, out of a total of 149. The Conservative Party finds its support chiefly among the large land owners and the commercial classes in the towns and cities.

The other parties bear the titles of Liberal Lefts, Radical Lefts, Social Democrats, Communists, Justice Union and Slesvig Party.

The Liberal Lefts represent the large-scale peasants or Gaardmaend.

The Radical Lefts represent the Husmaend, while the Social Democratic Party, which is the largest single group, represent a combination of the Husmaend, agricultural workers and artisans in both towns and country.

Following the election of 1932 the strength of these parties in the two houses of parliament was as follows:

	FOLKETING	LANDSTING
Liberal Lefts	38	28
Conservatives	27	13
Social Democrats	62	27
Radical Lefts	14	7
Justice Union	4	0

	FOLKETING	LANDSTING
Slesvig Party	1	0
Independent (elected on the Faroe Islands)	0	1
Communists	2	0

It is interesting to note that in a country predominantly agrarian the Social Democratic Party should be the largest single party having 62 members out of 149 in the popular branch of parliament and 27 out of 76 in the upper branch. It is of further interest to find that the followers of Henry George advocating the taxation of land values should have elected 4 members of the popular branch of parliament.

The present Ministry is made up from the more radical groups. Thus in 1934 the ministry of eleven members contained eight Social Democrats and three Radical Lefts. In other words it came exclusively from the small farmer or husmaend and the artisan classes of the country and the towns.

The cities reflect the same advanced opinions. In Copenhagen the Social Democratic party is in the majority having 35 seats out of 55.

The essential democracy of the country is further seen in the powers which local communities, towns and cities enjoy. They have almost complete control over everything that affects their own welfare. They are little republics within their proper sphere of action. They ask themselves as to what should be done, and once that is decided on, it can be done almost as quickly as by a private individual. Local government is almost the complete reverse of local government in America. Our towns and cities have only such limited powers as are given them by the state. They cannot own or operate a water plant, an electric light plant, a bus line, a garbage disposal plant; they cannot do their work by direct labor or control business or property save as the state permits it to be done if it permits it to be done at all. Moreover in Denmark the courts cannot be appealed to as to any action taken by parliament, by a city, by a town, by a county or even by a township. A private individual or a private corporation cannot question the sovereignty of the nation or even of a city or of a town. The courts have no political power. They are merely civil agencies to administer justice.

Thus we have a country in which neither the king nor the courts have any positive power over legislation or administration. The people themselves are the rulers and by their own choice they have come to rule through the social democratic party.

All this has come about by discussion; by discussion in the towns and villages, in the coöperative meetings; in the Folk High Schools, in the trade unions and in every group in the nation. There have been no revolutions; no appeals to force. The nation has trusted its liberties and its property without reservation to the majority will. And the result has been to lift the standard of living of all classes, and in lifting those at the botom it has lifted those above as well. This inherent intelligence and sense of justice of the people is one of the important things that the experience of Denmark discloses. It is not her economic gains alone, it is the latent power which lies hidden in the great mass of the people, that is the significant thing about this little country.

Nor have the gains been only of political and an economic sort. They are cultural as well. Illiteracy has been wiped out. It has been reduced to but .002 per cent. But the ending of illiteracy is not the significant thing about the culture of the country. That lies in the widespread intelligence of the people, an intelligence that includes an interest in literature and art, a familiarity with scientific things and a knowledge of international affairs from which Denmark has voluntarily chosen to be free.

CHAPTER XXII

A DEMOCRATIC BUDGET

THE first test of a government is who pays the bills and how and for what the money is spent. A government budget is an index of democracy or the reverse. Wherever the government is in the hands of privileged classes, there we find taxes on consumption to predominate. Wherever we find taxes levied upon incomes, inheritance and wealth there we find an approach to democracy.

Again we see the essential democracy of Denmark in the kind of taxes that are levied and especially in the things for which they are spent. In the first place Denmark approximates a free trade country. And many Danes regret that the aggressive nationalism of the world has forced their country to adopt higher customs taxes than were previously employed, although these rates are still relatively low.[1]

[1] The traditional tariff policy of Denmark has undergone a change in connection with the controlled economy designed to stabilize the national currency through the improvement of the credit balance. Increased duties have been levied on so-called articles of luxury in an effort to curtail their importation. The importation of automobiles is not encouraged for

Despite the fact that Denmark is an agricultural country, which we would expect to place a heavy customs tax on agricultural products, we find that animals and animal products, feeding stuffs, seeds, grain and mill produce, fertilizers as well as other garden and field produce are with certain exceptions exempt from duty. As to grain products, certain minimum prices are now maintained by means of a sliding scale of duties.

Spirits are taxed heavily and the duty on beer is high. Rates on tobacco and cigarettes have been recently increased.

Even at the present time, however, the average custom duties are only in the neighborhood of 10 per cent, having been increased from an average of 5 per cent in the pre-war years. The tariff is still largely a tariff for revenue rather than for protection and only a small amount of protection is provided by it.

Out of the total receipts of $92,421,000 the receipts from custom taxes are $22,140,000. Excise taxes are mainly imposed on spirits, on beer, on cigars and cigarettes. There are further consumption taxes on beet sugar, on coffee substitutes, on gasoline as well as a sales tax on chocolate. There is also an entertainment tax. All told the revenue from customs and excise taxes amounts to $58,860,000 or 63.7 per cent of the total revenues. Taxes on income and

various reasons. A sales tax is levied on autombiles varying from 15 per cent to 40 per cent of the value while some other duties with a similar purpose are levied.

property yield about $34,830,000 or 37 per cent of the total revenues. There is a real estate tax for national as well as local purposes. The income tax is levied upon personal incomes and the profits of corporations. The first $135 of the assessable income pays ½ of one per cent, the rate rising gradually into the higher brackets until an income of $250,000 pays 25 per cent. The corporation tax is assessed upon profits in excess of 5 per cent on the capital, the rate rising from 7 per cent to a little over 15 per cent. The corporation tax is a double tax, as the dividends are also taxed in the hands of the shareholder.

In addition there is a legacy duty on inherited estates which rises with the size of the legacy and the degree of kinship.

An even more impressive exhibit of the essential democracy of the country is seen in the things for which revenues are spent. Out of an annual budget of $90,215,000, only $11,700,000 or about 13 per cent of all expenditures is for national defense. The balance of the budget is for domestic services. The amount for social insurance, etc., amounts to $19,-030,000 or 21.1 per cent of the total. The expenditure for public education amounts to $18,090,000 or 20 per cent. The expenditure for health is $4,131,000 or 4.6 per cent.

Contributions by the central government alone for old age pensions amount to $9,450,000 or only $2,250,000 less than the total expenditure for military and naval defense, while the expenditure for unemployment, grants to sick and burial funds increase this item to $15,930,000.

The financial arrangements of the local authorities reflect the same democratic principles that prevail in the national budget. There is a municipal income tax as well as a national income tax. The former permits an exemption of $250.00 for the taxpayer and an additional allowance of $25.00 for every child in the family. The total revenues of all municipal authorities in 1932 amounted to $113,-535,000 of which $45,846,000 came from the income tax.

In the same year the local authorities derived $23,-949,000 from various kinds of municipal properties including public utilities owned by them.

The income tax is carried even down to the country districts. Out of a total of $46,332,000 of rural taxes $14,823,000 came from income taxes.

Out of a total of local expenditures for all purposes of $100,305,000, the expenditures for social purposes amounted to $27,810,000 or more than one-fourth of the total. This includes public relief, amounting to $10,800,000; expenditure for old age pensions amounting to $6,750,000; relief funds amounting to $4,735,000 and expenditure on unemployment of $2,565,000.

The local expenditure for public education amounts to $14,850,000.

So far as I know there is no country in which expenditures come as near to being for proper ends and collected from those best able to bear them as in Denmark. And much as other countries make use of the taxing power in the interest of special privileges, so Denmark makes use of the same power to free the nation from oppressive monopolies, to break up large estates by means of taxation and to place the burdens of government on incomes and wealth.

CHAPTER XXIII

HOUSING IN DENMARK
AND SWEDEN

"THERE are no slums in Copenhagen," is a statement that is often heard. There is relatively little over-crowding. Compared with the average large cities of America or Europe, there is no over-crowding at all.

Better housing for the poor is a problem to which western Europe is turning its attention. In some countries, as in Great Britain, the problem is being solved by municipal housing while in the Scandinavian countries the solution is a mixed one through state aid and through coöperative associations.

In Denmark, as in other countries, high costs prevailing during the war checked building operations. This resulted in a scarcity of dwellings. In Copenhagen there has been considerable building activity since 1916, in part by the municipality and by coöperative societies, in part by private enterprise aided by the municipality and the state. In the eighteen years from 1916 to 1934, 11,500 city owned flats were built, while an additional 31,700 flats were erected with governmental or municipal support, or a total of 43,200 in all. House building has been especially active since 1930. All told, in the twenty-two years from 1911 to 1933 about 83,000 flats were built. As in Sweden, the coöperative movement has entered the field of housing, more than 20,000 coöperative houses or apartments having been built in recent years. In 1911 the average number of persons per flat was 3.52. The number has now been reduced to 2.92. In other words, over-crowding is largely ended.

As in Sweden, the Danish coöperatives have introduced economies and services. It has sought to build as perfect apartments and houses as possible; also to build them at the lowest possible cost. The Workmen's Coöperative Building Society of Copenhagen had, as early as 1917, built 600 model flats at a total cost of $1,250,000. In connection with its construction projects it owns its own brickworks, which have proved very profitable. It also casts its own pipes, bricks, tile, etc. Cement is provided from a coöperative cement works, while the credit for its building operations is obtained through the Danish Coöperative Bank.

The Garden City Coöperative in Copenhagen acquired land from the city for 420 houses, the land reverting to the municipality at its cost price after the year 2000, by which procedure the unearned increment is retained by the municipality. This Society has built one-family houses, with good sized gardens to each house.

All apartment houses and tenements are built under strict municipal supervision insuring health and recreational facilities. There are large court-yards with adequate playing space for children. Also trees, plants and vegetation. Rents are still relatively high for the working classes, who pay rents representing from 20 per cent to 30 per cent of their income. Public assistance is granted those who because of unemployment or other reasons are unable to pay an economic rent. Rents in Copenhagen, for a small but modern two room flat, including central heating and hot water, range from 660 kroner to 850 kroner per year. Rents for flats of corresponding size in old houses range from 400 kroner to 450 kroner.

As a stimulus to building land values are kept down to a reasonable level, partly through the ownership of building sites by the city and partly through a requirement that the cost of land on which assisted building takes place should be correspondingly low. In other words, the city discourages land speculation and refuses to aid private builders who seek high profits from this source.

During the post-war period from 1918 to 1922 when building costs were abnormal the city and the government made direct subsidies on new buildings. Since 1922, however, public aid has been in the form of guaranteed loans which permit of cheap financing. Rents are kept down to cover costs. At the present time public assistance is only given to public utility societies. The local authorities appoint one representative on the governing committee of each society. He is required to attend all meetings; may take part in discussions but has no right of vote. In 1933 the state made a total sum of 30,000,000 kroner available in aid of housing.

Sweden has made the most outstanding contribution to coöperative housing. In Stockholm more than 15 per cent of a population of 500,000 already live in coöperative apartment houses. The procedure followed is to require a down payment of 5 per cent for low-cost apartments and 10 per cent for a high-cost apartment. As for the lowest economic group no down deposit is required at all, the state and city authorities providing the entire capital.

The coöperatively built houses have a quality of their own, different from those built by the state or by private capital. In the first place architects have had a freer hand in their designs. They have permitted their imaginations to play with the aim of securing both beauty and conveniences. This is especially true of the houses in Stockholm. Sites are carefully chosen; the building area is ample; rooms are equipped with modern convenience. There are provisions for radio sets and electrical kitchen appliances. There are group laundries and nurseries. In the large apartment houses gymnasiums are found.

Tenants in the coöperative apartments make their purchases at wholesale. Skilled designers provide modernistic furniture.

Reference has previously been made to the fact that one feels that he is moving in a new world in the coöperative movement. It is in a world in which the lowest economic group thinks and plans for itself. One catches this note in Sweden in connection with housing, as one does in Vienna. There is a wide difference between public housing for the poor in England and coöperative housing for the poor in the Scandinavian countries. The former are for the most part dull, uninteresting, lacking in beauty, while the latter are inspired by a belief in the same right to beauty, color and the joy of living for the poor as for the rich. Efforts are made to provide conveniences, gadgets and services adjusted to those who work all day, who have no servants and who have to add domestic work to their daily working responsibilities.

In fifteen years' time Sweden has spent $90,000,-000 on low-cost housing. In Stockholm alone apartments have been provided for some 65,000 people.

There is much suggestive of the housing of the future in what is known as the "Magic House" started in Stockholm in 1926. The "Magic House" is an intelligent adaption of all of the potential factors of present day housing. These factors include: (1) the use of low-cost and properly developed land in the suburbs, (2) the partial use of the "prefabricated house", and (3) permission to the buyer to contribute his own labor and the labor of his friends to so much of the building as is possible. In other words, Sweden is building houses much as did the American pioneer, with the addition of such contributions as industrialized society and public credit are able to add.

That this is a natural formula is shown by the fact that in less than ten years under this plan comfortable homes have been provided for more than 50,000 people and probably at a lower cost than any other housing scheme yet devised.

The procedure in connection with the "Magic House" is as simple as is the formula. The would-be house owner fills out an application blank setting forth the nature of his employment, his income, size of his family, etc. Those familiar with out-of-door work and mechanics are preferred. Also those whose incomes are less than $1300.00 a year. Preference is also given to those living in the more crowded districts.

As a guarantee of purpose the applicant makes a down payment of $80.00. In addition, and this is highly important, he contributes labor towards the erection of the house amounting to about $270.00, which covers the rough building operations of the cellar, framing, cement and other work. Skilled mechanics are employed for the interior work, finish, plumbing, electricity, etc. This amounts to approximately $270.00 more. The financing is through a loan from the city, the loan being protected by a first mortgage on the house. This loan approximates 90 per cent of the estimated cost of the house alone.

Like the farm settlements of Denmark the city owns the land and leases it for sixty years to the builder, permission being given for the transfer of the house by sale or otherwise. There is a ground rent charge payable to the city at 5 per cent of the value of the land.

Building lots are sufficiently large to provide for the growing of some vegetables and flowers with a small lawn. The usual size of the better types of suburban holdings is 75 x 100 square feet. In addition generous areas are laid apart for public parks, for play grounds, for swimming pools.

The Swedish "Magic House" is a great advance on public housing in England and on the continent in other ways. Electricity is cheap in Scandinavia and the houses make provisions for its generous use. There is a bath, toilet, central heating plant, gas stoves, and city water. All this equipment has been standardized for easy installation. About 60 per cent of these small houses have garages.

The "Magic House" is economically sound. During the depression only two of such houses were sold at sheriff's sale. The householder is held to a strict payment of his obligations. In the aggregate, in the year 1934, the real estate department of the city of Stockholm reported a surplus of 817,000 kroner on its operations which went into the city surplus for that year.

While it may be true that the Scandinavian people have a greater aptitude for this sort of thing than have our own and greater permanence of residence, the economic factors and human qualities of people are much the same. And I think the hunger for a home to which one contributes his own work and his own imagination is universal as to all people. The following description of what happens to the prospective owner of a "Magic House" is taken from "Sweden: The Middle way" by Marquis W. Childs:

"When the contract is finally signed, there is tremendous excitement in the family of the prospective home owner. They have leased the lot and made a first payment on the materials for a house, and now it is up to them to build it. Early and late the whole family works, and brothers and cousins and uncles volunteer their services, somewhat after the fashion of a middle-western barn-raising. First the cellar must be dug, following the careful instructions contained in the handbook provided by the city. If difficulties, such as rock requiring blasting, are encountered, the city takes over and prorates the added cost among all the houses, so that no one individual is penalized. When the excavation is completed, the aerated blocks for construction of the basement wall are delivered and the prospective householder turns mason, under the supervision of inspectors employed by the city. Because the basement is used for food storage, bathroom, laundry, workroom, and garage, great care is taken in waterproofing the foundation.

"On every side 'Magic Houses' are going up. The head of the household comes direct from his work to the site of the new house. The older children may be there already, prepared to help or merely to become acquainted with the new neighborhood. In the late afternoon the wife arrives with a hamper of lunch and the whole family has a picnic supper on the site where the house will rise. Nearby are other similar groups, and children and grownups strike up early friendships with future neighbors.

"The joists and the flooring arrive from the factory all cut to exact size and numbered in accord with the detailed plan that the householder must follow. When the foundation work is completed, the ready-made wooden wall sections are installed and here expert workmen are usually required. Experts are needed in most instances, too, for the installation of electric wiring, water pipes, and plumbing fixtures and to do the sheet-iron and glazing work. As the work progresses through the summer and early fall, numerous small tasks fall to the lot of the children. The wife, too, does her share, with a paint-brush or even a hammer and a saw. At last the head of the household in on top of the roof laying the tiles. The weather stripping is all in place. The instructor, who has checked up on every detail as construction has gone forward, will come only once more. The kitchen cabinet, closet, and shelves, all finished at the factory, have been installed and a housewarming is close at hand. The

"Magic House" has taken shape in a few short months under the eyes of the family that will occupy it." [1]

[1] See "Sweden: The Middle Way," page 63.

CHAPTER XXIV

PROVISIONS FOR SOCIAL SECURITY

UNLESS it be Soviet Russia, I fancy there is no country that has made as complete provision for human security as has Denmark. This has been done in an orderly and exact way. The problem has been approached in two ways: first, by enabling the individual to provide for his own security, and, second, where that is inadequate or impossible, provision is made for such security by the State. The program begins with the easy facility of land settlement, with a completely equipped homestead where a man can work out his own salvation, supplemented by the helpful services provided by the coöperative movement. This has been described elsewhere. In addition there are various kinds of insurance funds, and other aids through social legislation.

One would not expect an agricultural country to show great concern for the wage workers of the cities. Yet Denmark has carried social legislation further and into more diverse fields than any country with which I am acquainted. As a result, it is possible to say that "there is no poverty in Denmark". Possibly it is safer to say there is no *la misere*. Not only is the number and percentage of persons in the lowest economic scale relatively small, but those who have lost out in the game of life are cared for more solicitously and intelligently than in any other nation of Western Europe, if not in the world.

Denmark is a pioneer in social legislation, the beginnings having been made in the nineties of the last century. During the present century, with the advent of a Social Democratic government, a number of advanced measures have been enacted covering almost every phase of social security. The demands of the Social Democratic party were embodied into law in 1933 in the form of a social code. The outstanding features of this code are the following:

(1) Proper hygienic and sanitary conditions are required for all workshops. Children under fourteen are prohibited from working in any handicraft, while between the ages of fourteen and nineteen night work is prohibited.

(2) For four weeks after childbirth women may not work in a factory unless possessed of a medical certificate to the effect that there is no danger to the health of the mother or child. During this period the mother may receive public assistance in case she is not entitled to confinement assistance provided in the social insurance and sick clubs.

(3) Under the widows' pensions act, which became effective January 1, 1914, every widow who is

the mother of a child or children under 14, whose property and income is less than a certain amount proportionate to the size of her family, is entitled to a public grant toward the support of her family. The amount of assistance varies according to the age of the children, the highest allowance being made for children under two years of age. In exceptional cases the aid may be extended till the child is 18 years of age. The grants are not pauperizing; in fact the purpose is to avoid this very thing. They are given only to mothers who measure up to a certain standard of fitness and whose homes are proper places for bringing up children. They are conditional upon the mother's not becoming a subject of public charity. Half the expense involved in these widows' pensions is borne by the state and the rest by the community in which the widow lives.[1]

For each child under two the widowed mother receives $40.00 a year as state aid. For each child between four and twelve and fourteen the allowance is $24.00 per annum.

(4) The eight-hour day has been almost universal since 1919 through voluntary agreements between employers and workmen. Night work is prohibited in some industries.

(5) A great advance has been made in the prevention of strikes. Since as early as 1899 arbitration

[1] United States Department of Labor, Children's Bureau, "Laws Relating to Mothers' Pensions in the United States, Denmark and New Zealand." Bureau publication No. 7.

of industrial disputes has been general. A permanent arbitration court serves as a tribunal for the settlement of disputes regarding collective agreements. These laws have been so successful that in 1931 there were but 16 and in 1932 but 17 labor stoppages in the country. Whereas the working days lost in 1919 amounted to 900,000, in 1920 to 1,300,000, and in 1922 to 2,300,000, the loss in 1932 was reduced to but 87,000.

The program of social legislation referred to comprises three major insurance Acts, and an Act regarding public assistance. The three insurance Acts provide for (1) Unemployment insurance, (2) Accident insurance, and (3) National insurance, the latter combining sickness, invalidity and old-age insurance.

Sickness insurance is especially widespread. Each Sick Club is a separate unit. In rural areas the unit covers an entire parish, while in urban areas the insured person is free to select his own society.

Sickness insurance is not designed exclusively for workmen. It is open to all men and women of similar economic standing, and includes small farmers, agricultural workers, civil servants, and the like. Two-thirds of the population are insured against sickness through these local agencies operating under general State supervision. The insurance provides the members with free hospital treatment, cash benefits, medical aid, as well as maternity benefits.

The administration of unemployment insurance

is closely interlocked with the trades unions, who require their members to be insured against unemployment. As approximately 85% of all workers are organized, the unemployment insurance scheme is on a voluntary basis and practically universal.

Compensation of workmen for injuries is compulsory, the employers in this case being responsible for the entire cost of the insurance. The Act covers not only workers in all trades but also any and all persons who do work for others. The Labor Insurance Board decides all questions of liability.

The number of persons receiving benefits annually through these various insurance schemes range from 300,000 to 400,000. The great majority of these would have been required to seek public help had they not been protected in this way.

Again as to other institutions of Denmark, statistics tell only a part of the story. They indicate, however, the burden borne by the people, the number of persons aided, and the misfortunes or accidents which are covered by social legislation and insurance.

First, the population of Denmark is 3,600,000.

The administration of social legislation is extremely decentralized. It is carried back to the neighborhood. There are 22 county districts. These districts are again divided into 87 urban district areas and 1,300 rural areas.

Utilizing these administrative agencies are 1,650 Sickness Benefit Societies or Sick Clubs which have a total membership of approximately 1,950,000 persons who are protected against illness, invalidity and old age.

There are 70 Approved Unemployment Societies with a membership of approximately 300,000, while 900,000 wage earners are insured against accident under the workmen's compensation scheme.

The expenditure for benefits is as follows for the year 1931:

The benefits paid out through the Sickness Benefit Societies or Sick Clubs amounted to 47,500,000 Kroner, of which some 32,000,000 Kroner were derived from contributions from members, while State grants amounted to 11,000,000 Kroner, municipal grants to about 500,000 Kroner, the balance being derived from other sources.

In the same year, the sum paid in the form of invalidity pensions totaled 15,000,000 Kroner, of which 6,100,000 Kroner were received from members' contributions, while employers contributed 3,-600,000 Kroner, the State and local authorities being responsible for the balance.

Old age pensions involved in that year an expenditure of 60,000,000, of which the State paid 35,-000,000 Kroner and municipal authorities 25,000,000 Kroner, all of the contributions being from public authorities.

Unemployment insurance, covering approximately 300,000 wage earners, involved an expenditure of about 25,700,000 Kroner with respect to normal and extraordinary unemployment relief only. Of this total sum the State granted 4,900,000 Kroner and local authorities 4,200,000 Kroner, the balance being provided by the members.

In addition to the above, in 1932-1933, the unemployment insurance and other unemployment benefits paid aggregated 100,000,000 Kroner, of which the members contributed 32,000,000 Kroner, the State 39,000,000 Kroner, local authorities 29,000,000 Kroner, and employers 4,000,000 Kroner.

CHAPTER XXV

AN ALTERNATIVE TO
SOCIALISM

DENMARK draws what seems to be a natural line between those things that can be done best by the state and those things that can be best done by individuals or by voluntary association. The state owns the steam railways, the postal service, the telegraph and the trunk lines of the telephone service between the different towns and provinces, the local telephone service being in the hands of private companies with a government concession. In North Sleswig, however, the local telephone service is run by the province. The telephone is almost universal in the country there being one for every three families and the rates are low. In the towns and cities the public utilities are generally owned by the local authorities.

An overwhelming part of the fire insurance business is covered by three long established mutual companies. One was founded in 1731, another in 1761, and the third in 1792.

Life insurance, sickness and accident insurance

are likewise largely covered by mutual societies. Almost all insurance relating to domestic animals is mutual. All told, there are approximately 200 mutual insurance companies in the country which in 1932 did a gross business of $17,280,000.

The railways are divided into two groups. The main lines of about 2,500 kilometers belong to the state while the branch lines of merely local importance with 2,600 kilometers are privately owned. The phrase "private" in Denmark, must be taken with a large reservation. It means something quite different when applied to the railways or telephones of Denmark than when applied to the railways or telephones of America. The private lines are run by private companies but nearly all the capital belongs to the state and the towns, hardly any private capital being invested in them.

The total capital invested in railways in 1932 amounted to $152,000,000 or $30,000 per mile.

One sees how many transportation, industrial and farm problems solve themselves with the railways in public hands. There are no conflicts over regulation, no such agencies as Inter-State Commerce Commissions, State Railway Commissions and no controversy in and out of parliament. The railroads are operated for service. They are almost like the elevators in a building. If they lose money as they do, no one is greatly concerned for some one has enjoyed a compensating gain in low freight or in passenger service. The railroads might in fact be operated free and all save a fraction of the operating costs would come back to the people and especially to the farmer in services rendered. He would save it in costs on his exports as he would save it on his imports.

In the year 1933 there was a loss on the public undertakings amounting to $12,960,000, almost all of which, or $11,340,000 was chargeable to the railways. In this deficit, however, are included both interest and sinking fund charges, as well as contributions towards the cost of the pension system for the employees.

Not only are the railways operated as agencies of service and especially of service to the exporting farmers but railway expansion has been used to develop the more sparsely populated portions of the country. This has resulted in an increase in population as well as in the economic up-building of the nation.

Great steam ferries have been built and equipped to carry passenger and freight trains across arms of the sea without trans-shipment. Some of these ferries ply across waters where the sea is often very rough. Some ferries are large enough to carry two sets of tracks.

These ferries are all good sea-boats, are fast and steady. By means of them a through mail route has been established from Sweden and Norway with the rest of Europe.

The passenger rates on Danish railroads were,

until 1903 at least, very low as compared with those of other countries. It is difficult to make a comparison, because many of the countries in Europe have been experimenting to increase passenger service by low rates of fare, by week-end trips, by circular tours about the country and by otherwise encouraging commercial and recreational travel.

In 1903 Danish first class railway fares were exactly one-half the fares in Prussia; second class which is widely used was 40 per cent of the Prussian rate while third class was a little more than one-third of the rate in the latter country.

One of the devices for increasing travel are season tickets which are sold for use on all railroads on which one can travel as often and as far as one wishes. Thus a season ticket, good for eight days, costs 52.50 kroner for first class fare and 35 kroner for third class fare. A ticket good for fifteen days costs 75 kroner and third class 50 kroner. Over 96 per cent of the passengers travel third class.

Freight rates were relatively even lower on comparable commodities.

Transportation charges are definitely fixed with service uppermost. Rates and fares are officially fixed so that (1) they will aid in the economic development of the country and (2) so that they decrease rapidly per mile as the distance increases.

A commission created to consider principles which should govern railroad administration which reported in 1903 stated: "The geographical lie of the provinces—the position of the country preventing the development of transit traffic—the poverty of Denmark in minerals, which elsewhere provide a lucrative source of traffic; and lastly the obligation in the true interest of civilization to construct railways through poor districts, are circumstances that have always been so imbued in the minds of legislators that it has been necessary to recognize how difficult it is to calculate on the state railways bringing in 4, 3½, or even 3%."

In keeping with these principles a system of profit-sharing was proposed in the hope that the employees would be stimulated to improve the administration and bring about economies in operation.

In 1926 radio broadcasting was taken over by the state. In the year 1933-34 the number of registered receiving sets were 548,000 while the receipts of the state broadcasting agency, collected mostly from licenses and taxes on receiver sets, was $1,431,-000.00 with an expenditure of $1,215,000.00.

The other major industry of the country, which with transportation, exercises the greatest power is that of banking and credit. There is but one bank of issue, the Rigsbanken or National Bank. It is administered by five directors of whom two are appointed by the Crown. It has five branches in different parts of the country. While the bank is "private" in name, it is subject to very complete oversight and control by the two government appointees. In addition the state has a prior claim on the earnings of the bank. Of the annual profits, 750,000 kroner first go to the state. The balance is divided according to fixed rules between the state, the reserve fund and the shareholders.

Mortgage institutions like insurance are mutual or coöperative. The mortgage credit societies are designed to provide cheap credit and at the same time insure satisfactory security. The societies are associations of borrowers, organized with joint liability on the members to provide credit to one another. These societies work within local districts. In 1932 there were 13 of such institutions with outside loans of 4,185,000,000 kroner. The great bulk of these loans were at 4½ per cent. In addition to these associations the cities have joined together and organized a Mortgage Credit Society which in 1931 had bonds in circulation to the amount of 120,000,000 kroner.

In America there is indignant protest against "regimentation" on the part of the state and a clamor that business be freed from governmental intrusion and competition. Here is a little country, certainly as democratic as our own, certainly as individualistic as any country in the world, and prizing its individualism as do few countries, yet it has carried its control of private capitalism further than any country in the world unless it be Russia. On the one hand is the coöperative movement through which from 80 to 90 per cent of the products of the farm are manufactured, processed and sold through coöperative societies. By the same devices the farmer buys his fertilizer, his seeds and his farm implements and distributes them back to the consumer. In the realm of merchandising there are 1824 societies organized as coöperatives which buy and distribute from 17 to 20 per cent of the total volume of consumer's goods covered by the coöperatives. In this realm of merchandising there are wholesale associations which minister to the local associations as well as export societies which carry Danish bacon, Danish butter and Danish eggs to the consumer in England. This is but a part of the collective life of Denmark in this field.

Wherever it is possible for individuals to act through voluntary associations this procedure is followed. Wherever voluntary coöperation is impossible and a responsible control of an industry is necessary it is in the hands of the state.

Thus comparatively little is left to private capitalism in the major activities in the country and that little is watchfully controlled by the state or by the coöperative societies. Added to this is the conscious use of taxation as a means of preventing monopoly or minimizing its power. There are practically no protective tariffs to encourage local industry. This insures free competition within the country. Even those privileges identified with the land are being progressively broken down, first by the purchase of the estates and their division among the people, and second by the taxation of land values in a way that bears heavily on the great estate owners and tends to force them to dispose of their holdings to those who are better able to use them by intensive cultivation.

Decade by decade democracy is enveloping private capitalism and transferring it either to coöperative societies or to the state. Each step is taken after mature deliberation and discussion as each new undertaking is tested out and absorbed into the life of the nation.

As in Sweden the Danes have attacked the trust and monopoly by direct action. When an industry which supplied goods necessary to farmers threatened to combine or to impose conditions which were considered unfair or unreasonable, the farmers organized to create a society of their own to supply the goods on coöperative lines, thereby delivering the most effective counter-stroke possible to the attempt to impose high prices upon them. They effected their ends first by withdrawing their custom from the monopoly and second by establishing a plant of their own. By this means they were able to fix fair prices to all buyers.

CHAPTER XXVI

A STUDY IN POLITICAL CONTRASTS

As compared with Denmark, democracy is a land into which we have not been permitted to enter. With us democracy is jug-handled; it is hobbled by our inflexible constitutions, by the limitations on the powers of the nation and the states, and by the all but complete lack of liberty of action on the part of our towns and cities. Only those who have had actual experience with legislation and administration in America know the extent and costs of these obstructions; costs that are social as well as financial. Not only is the government very limited in its powers, but the procedure to be followed is made as difficult as possible by constitutional and legal provisions and especially by the thousands of decisions by the courts, each of which becomes a governing rule which must be observed by every agency of the government even though the rule was laid down a century ago.

Democracy in America is the reverse of that of Denmark. With us democracy has been built on distrust; distrust of the executive, distrust of the legislature, distrust of the people. This distrust has been heightened by the extreme legalism of our institutions; a legalism which has been taken advantage of by the lawyers and by the courts, which have written new restrictions and new limitations on the state. As a people we are in a political jungle of legalism, the effect of which is to make government devious, costly, difficult, at times unworkable.

I know of no country in which government has to work under as many handicaps and with as many obstacles to be overcome as does America.

Denmark is free from all these things; so free in fact that it seems almost incredible that a people could trust themselves so completely. There are no inhibitions as to the things the people may do. There is apparently but one rule. That is, that when the people act, by their votes, the Government shall carry that decision into effect and shall do so with the minimum of delay. In other words, the Government is completely responsible to the will of the people. And it is responsible to no one else.

When one examines the operations of such a system, one sees that there is little that democracy can do that is injurious to the state, to the majority of the people or even to any save a privileged few. In the long run majorities can only legislate in the interest of the majority. Public opinion takes care of this. As to minorities, the only thing democracy can do is to take from them special privileges they have acquired through the control of the government. Even property is fully protected; especially such property as is created by labor. It is as secure under democracy as it is under any form of Government.

There are further facts about the political life of Denmark that are so different from other countries that it is difficult to define them. One is the intimacy of the people with politics. Political thought and action is going on all the time, almost as naturally as the day's work. The people are related to the Government as though it belongs to them, is a part of them, something to be freely used by them. The relationship is not dissimilar from that within the co-operative movement. This is true as to national as it is to local affairs.

One explanation of this is the feeling of assurance with which people act. There are no prohibitions of any kind on such action. Should they decide that the city should own a public utility that is the end of it. Should they feel that all labor disputes should be arbitrated, they know that this will be done if enough people want it done. If they are opposed to the spending of money for the army and navy, they are able to end it. Taxes, too, can be placed where the people feel they should be placed, while the railroads, the telephones and the other public utilities can be made to conform to any regulations which the people may desire.

This immediate responsiveness of government to the will of the people is, in my opinion, an explanation of the interest taken by the people in the government. And there is no way of knowing how much of our own failure is due to the fact that we operate under entirely different conditions; conditions which palsy enthusiasm as they palsy effort. Every decision of the people and every decision of a town, a city, a State, or the Federal Government, is merely a tentative decision. It has no finality. It must pass scrutiny by the courts. If it involves social legislation or any property interest, it is most surely likely to be halted by the courts. Not by the Supreme Court at Washington alone but by any one of thousands of courts that see fit to suspend the operation of a law or an administrative decision under the law. This, I think, is one reason why men of ability do not enter or remain in American politics. They enter office with the expectation of using their powers for some public good. They find that their efforts are blocked by court decisions and that years may pass before the question is finally settled. They find their enthusiasms chilled by their helplessness. And they retire to private affairs where their abilities and efforts will realize results. The same is true of reform organizations as it is true of individuals.[1]

[1] The recent decisions and orders of the federal courts suspending the execution of Acts of Congress, as well as the continuing decisions and orders of both state and federal courts directed to regulatory agencies and public authorities, have established the fact that it is almost impossible for a single Congress, the President with a four-year term, or any city administration to carry into execution any measure affecting

A second fact of significance is the aptitude of the people for political life, especially of those classes which we generally distrust. Denmark has found ability among men who are low in the economic scale. Many such men, who know only the work of a small farm, have exhibited as much constructive statesmanship as have those from the top.

Finally it is significant that democracy has not been accompanied with dishonesty, with the spoils system, with the use of power for private ends. This is true as to all classes in Denmark. It is due in part to the fact that so many persons are looking on. The closeness of politics to the life of the people and the responsiveness of the officials to public opinion is in itself an assurance of honesty.

Denmark differs again from other countries in that it is ruled by farmers. Only to a limited extent have the commercial and industrial classes shared in the government. They have never been a majority power. In other words, Denmark is a producers' state. And it is ruled by the producers. Legislation is in the interest of the producing class as is the press, the educational agencies and the public opinion of the country.

propertied or privileged interests which such interests oppose. During the last two years over 2,000 restraining orders and injunctions have been issued against various agencies of the federal government alone, which orders, with the delays incident to them, have put in suspense scores of recovery projects which were required to wait for months and even years upon the opinions of one or more of the courts of the nation.

The economic democracy of Denmark is a product of political democracy, and this economic democracy is as challenging to our assumptions as is her political life. There are no multi-millionaires in the country. They seem not to be necessary. There are no privileged classes. Instead there is a uniformly high standard of living and a widespread equality of opportunity.

Denmark is a further exhibit of the relative ease with which all reasonable wants can be satisfied, and the high standard of living that is possible when that which is produced is equitably distributed. The obstacles to such a distribution have been so completely removed that wealth finds its way to the user with a minimum of overhead costs. And a comparison of that country with our own discloses that the excessive overhead in America and the inequitable distribution of wealth are traceable to special privileges either created by legislation or directly issuing out of legislation.

Denmark is relatively free from such underholds.

First there is an approach to free trade. Monopoly has been all but destroyed by opening up the buyers' market to the competition of the world. It has brought to the Danes the best that the world produces and of the best quality. But this means the price has been kept close to the production cost. This policy has not resulted in a low standard of living for labor. The reverse is true. The standard of wages in Denmark is higher than in almost any country in

Europe, while the worker buys at a competitive cost. Denmark is an outstanding exhibit of the fact that wages are determined by other things than a protective tariff.

The second special privilege is the adjustment of taxation. And in Denmark the great bulk of the taxes are levied upon incomes and wealth rather than on consumption. This is true as to local as well as national taxes. From the bottom to the top, taxation is adjusted in large measure on the principle of ability to pay.

A third special privilege is that of transportation. And transportation in our country is intimately related to almost every other monopoly. Next to the tariff, it is the foster mother of monopoly. Despite legislation by the Federal and State governments, there are indiscoverable privileges and abuses connected with the railroads which contribute not only to a high cost of living but to monopoly as well.

The railroads of Denmark are operated very much like the elevators of a building. They are run with the aim of service. Rates on agricultural produce are very low. So also are passenger fares. Tickets are obtainable for one week or two weeks which permit one to travel ten miles or a thousand miles at the same price.

Like the railroads, the telegraph, the telephones and the local public utilities are either owned and operated for service at low cost or are under the most complete regulation and control by the State.

Possibly the most outstanding factors in the high standard of living and the quality of freedom of the country is the wide-spread ownership of the land and along with it the protection which the homesteader enjoys from the Government, or the coöperative societies of which he is a member. All save five per cent of the farmers are free-hold owners. The ease with which the tenant and the worker escape to the land is a major explanation of the sense of security of the average Dane as it is an explanation of the relatively high standard of living of the wage worker.

Denmark is no longer an experiment. Her democratic institutions are at least a generation old. Many have been operating for three-quarters of a century. They are as permanent a part of the life of the people as is the capitalistic system with us.

CHAPTER XXVII

FARM TENANCY IN AMERICA

DENMARK is not the only country in Europe that is taking steps to end farm landlordism. Possibly the changes taking place with respect to the land are more significant than those taking place with respect to industry. In some parts of Europe the old estates were seized by the peasants following the War and divided up into small holdings. In other countries the distribution of the land was by peaceful means. In Russia the land has been communalized and is being cultivated by large scale industrial methods. In Germany, even prior to the War, land was being acquired and divided into small holdings which were sold to the peasants, credit being provided by the state. It is in the smaller countries of Ireland, Denmark and Sweden, however, that this movement has become the outstanding program of the country. In Ireland, British legislation began to convert the tenant into an owner at the end of the last century. The Irish Free State has decreed, in effect, that all farm land should be owned by the occupier or temporarily by the government in process of ultimate distribution to peasant occupiers. In fact in practically every country of Northern Europe land tenure and land uses are being subject to change. As to how far this movement will go one can only speculate. That it has gone as far as it has and is approved of by so many different types of government is indicative of the significance of the movement.

A study of the census in America shows that we are fast creating old world conditions. Yet while Europe is recognizing the evils of tenancy and is taking steps to reduce it, little attention has as yet been given to the subject in this country. At the present rate of growth, every second farmer will be a tenant in a very short time, if this is not already true. More than 40% of our farmers were tenants in 1930.

Reports of the United States Census graphically disclose the rapidity of the change which is taking place. It shows this change decade by decade. Thus:

(1) In the 40 years from 1890 to 1930 the total number of farms increased from 4,564,641 in the former year to 6,288,648 in the latter.

(2) During these years farms operated by owners and managers increased from 3,269,728 to 3,624,283, an increase of 354,555, or about 11%; while

(3) During the same period the number of farms operated by tenants increased from 1,294,912

to 2,664,365, or an increase of more than 100%.

(4) In 1890, 28.4% of all farms were operated by tenants, while in 1930 the percentage was 43.4%.

Tenancy is highest in those parts of the country where it would be least expected—in the central, west and south. Thus we find (1930) the percentage of tenant-operated farms in the West South Central Division (Arkansas, Louisiana, Oklahoma, Texas) to be 62.3% of the total; in the East South Central Division (Kentucky, Tennessee, Alabama, Mississippi) to be 55.9%; in the South Atlantic (Delaware, Maryland, District of Columbia, Virginia, West Virginia, North Carolina, South Carolina, Georgia, Florida) to be 48.1%; in the West North Central (Minnesota, Iowa, Missouri, North Dakota, South Dakota, Nebraska, Kansas) to be 39.9%; in the East North Central (Ohio, Indiana, Illinois, Michigan, Wisconsin) to be 29.3%; in the Mountain Division (Montana, Idaho, Wyoming, Colorado, New Mexico, Utah, Nevada) to be 24.4%, while in the Pacific Division it is 17.7%.

In other words, tenancy is most pronounced in the middle and southern sections of the nation, including the South Atlantic and Gulf Seaboard states.

Tenancy is at its maximum in the following states: Mississippi, 72.2%; Georgia, 68.2%; Louisiana, 66.6%; South Carolina, 65.1%; Alabama, 64.7%;

Arkansas, 63.0%; Oklahoma, 61.5%; Texas, 60.9%; North Carolina, 49.2%; Iowa, 47.3%; Nebraska, 47.1%; Tennessee, 46.2%.

Commenting on the condition of the farm tenant, a Subcommittee of the House Committee on Public Lands of the 74th Congress says:

"Struggling against these tremendous odds, the American farmer is being driven into a condition of tenantry.

"Even now 3,000,000 farm families are settling down to a social state of serfdom heretofore foreign to our great country.

"Almost 2,000,000 more with their farm homes heavily mortgaged, struggle on under the burden of debt, hoping that a kind Providence will save them from a like fate.

"Less than 2,000,000 families of the nation's once proud group of independent home-owning farmers remain, and their ranks are thinning every year.

"The independent home owner is rapidly vanishing.

"It is evident that the present trend of agriculture is toward a system of tenantry and serfdom that is destructive of the liberty and freedom of the individual citizen and foreign to the doctrine of equality of citizenship.

"This condition is brought about largely by economic practices beyond the farmer's control and is very undesirable, both economically and socially, tending to destroy essential elements of our Christian civilization." [1]

In 1913 a study of agricultural tenancy was made by the Commission on Industrial Relations.

Speaking of the effect of tenancy on the tenant and the low standard of life which prevails among tenant farmers, the Commission states:

"Under this (the tenant) system tenants as a class earn only a bare living through the work of themselves and their entire families. Few of the tenants ever succeed in laying by a surplus. On the contrary, their experiences are so discouraging that they move from one farm to the next in the constant hope of being able to better their condition. Without the labor of the entire family the tenant farmer is helpless. As a result, not only is his wife prematurely broken down but the children remain uneducated and without the hope of any condition better than that of their parents. The tenants having no interest in the results beyond the crops of a single year, the soil is being rapidly exhausted and the conditions, therefore, tend to become steadily worse. Even at present a very large proportion of the tenants' families are insufficiently clothed, badly housed, and underfed. Practically all of the white tenants are native-born. As a result of these conditions, however, they are deteriorating rapidly, each generation being

[1] Report 74th Congress, 2nd session, on H.R. 8286, Government Printing Office (Wash.), D. C.

less efficient and more hopeless than the one preceding."

Continuing, the report says:

"The cost of tenancy is appalling. A large proportion of tenants are hopelessly in debt and are charged exorbitant rates of interest. Over 95 per cent of the tenants borrow from some source and about 75 per cent borrow regularly year after year. The average interest rate on all farm loans is 10 per cent, while small tenants in Texas pay 15 per cent or more. In Oklahoma the conditions are even worse in spite of the enactment of laws against usury. Furthermore, over 80 per cent of the tenants are regularly in debt to the stores from which they secure their supplies and pay exorbitantly for this credit. The average rate of interest on store credit is conservatively put at 20 per cent, and in many cases ranges as high as 60 per cent.

"The leases are largely in the form of oral contracts which run for only one year and which make no provision for compensation to the tenant for any improvements which may be made upon the property. As a result, tenants are restrained from making improvements, and in many cases do not properly provide for the up-keep of the property.

"Furthermore, the tenants are in some instances the victims of oppression on the part of landlords. This oppression takes the form of dictation of character and amount of crops, eviction without due notice, and discrimination because of personal and political convictions. The existing law provides no recourse against such abuses.

"As a result both of the evils inherent in the tenant system and of the occasional oppression by landlords, a state of acute unrest is developing among the tenants, and there are clear indications of the beginning of organized resistance which may result in civil disturbances of a serious character.

"The situation is being accentuated by the increasing tendency of the landlords to move to the towns and cities, relieving themselves not only from all productive labor but from direct responsibility for the conditions which develop. Furthermore, as a result of the increasing expenses incident to urban life there is a marked tendency to demand from the tenant a greater share of the products of his labor.

"The responsibility for the existing conditions rests not upon the landlords but upon the system itself. The principal causes are to be found in the system of short leases, the system of private credit at exorbitant rates, the lack of a proper system of marketing, the absence of educational facilities, and last but not least the prevalence of land speculation.

"A new factor is being introduced into the agricultural situation through the development of huge estates owned by corporations and operated by salaried managers upon a purely industrial system. The labor conditions on such estates are subject to grave criticism. The wages are extremely low, 80 cents per day being the prevailing rate on one large estate which was thoroughly investigated; arbitrary deductions from wages are made for various purposes; and a considerable part of the wages themselves are paid in the form of coupons, which are in all essential particulars the same as the 'scrip' which has been the source of such great abuse. Furthermore, the communities existing on these large estates are subject to the complete control of the landowning corporation, which may regulate the lives of citizens to almost any extent. There is an apparent tendency toward the increase of these large estates, and the greatest abuses may be expected if they are allowed to develop unchecked."

The evils of farm tenancy are being recognized in America no less than in Europe. At the last session of Congress a bill was introduced in the Senate known as the Bankhead Bill for the purpose of helping would-be farm tenants and share croppers to buy farm homes, being aided to do so by the government. The avowed purpose of the Act is to check the increase in farm tenancy, to alleviate conflicts between land owners and tenants, to protect soil resources, to promote more secure occupancy, and in general to return farms now occupied by tenants to freehold owners. These objects were to be promoted through a "Farm Tenants Homes Corporation" organized for the purpose. It was to be given power to acquire farm lands and personal property needed for the operation of farms; to develop and lease the property to farm tenants and share croppers; to accept mortgages to secure the payment; and otherwise to promote the transfer of tenant farmers into owners. In carrying out this project, the corporation was authorized to issue bonds not to exceed $1,000,000,000 in amount, in addition to a capital stock of not to exceed $100,000,000 to be subscribed by the Secretary of the Treasury.

Loans made under the Act are to be payable in not less than 30 and not more than 50 annual installments, payments to commence three years after the date the land is acquired. The rate of interest is to be as low as the corporation can secure plus a reasonable charge for administration.

The Bill passed the Senate but failed of consideration in the House.

CHAPTER XXVIII

THE COÖPERATIVE
MOVEMENT IN AMERICA

THE story of the humble beginnings of the coöperative movement in England has often been told. It had its birth among the poor weavers of Rochdale in December, 1844. It was born of a hope of realizing some small gains by the buying of goods and supplies at wholesale and their distribution to members at retail. The principles laid down by these humble weavers have been followed without substantial change, until today the movement encircles the world with a growth far more rapid and secure than at any time in the past. This is as true of America as it is of other countries.

Throughout the world the Consumers' Coöperative Movement has withstood the destructive winds of ninety years' experience, and has grown into tremendous economic organizations affecting the economic life of many countries. In Great Britain membership has steadily increased until at the end of last year it reached a record total of close to 7,000,-000. One-seventh of all goods consumed in England is sold by the consumers' coöperative movement through 10,000 retail coöperative stores. The English Coöperative Wholesale Society, organized in 1864, now has a capital of money and ships, lands and equipment of $450,000,000 and annual sales of more than $415,000,000. The total retail and wholesale trade amounts to almost $2,000,000,000. The coöperative banks have an annual turnover of more than $3,000,000,000. In 1933 the "Coöps" distributed to their consumer members over $100,000,000 in patronage dividends.

Switzerland has towns where every industry and utility is coöperative.

Over half of the people of Finland are already coöperative even though coöperation only started there at the turn of the century.

The Swedish Coöperatives report a total membership of over 500,000, an increase of 300,000 since 1918. They have over 4,000 local stores. A few years ago the Swedish coöperators broke the yoke of their flour, margarine, fertilizer and electric bulb cartels or trusts.

The International Coöperative Wholesale Society placed the world's largest orders on the London market for tea, coffee, and sugar in 1933.

Today consumers' coöperation is the largest democratic movement in the world, with over 100,000,-000 families, or 400,000,000 persons already members.

The first principle of the coöperative society was

one of simple democracy. The principle is "one person one vote," regardless of the number of shares one owns. Each member must cast his own vote, voting by proxy being usually forbidden, just as in a political democracy one must cast his own vote or he cannot vote at all. The coöperative is run for the benefit of the members and they have absolute control over it. A fixed and limited rate of interest may be paid on shares of capital. Shares cannot be sold for more than their face value. Finally, the profits, or more accurately, the surplus savings of the coöperative, are paid back to the consumer-producer-owners, not as dividends on the stock they own, but as dividends in proportion to their purchases or sale, so that those who have bought most or sell the most get the largest return.

In this country also consumers' coöperation came into being in the "hungry forties" of the last century. A group of working men's families opened the first coöperative store in Boston in 1845. The Riverhead Town Agricultural Society formed in 1863 was among the first of the farm purchasing or rural consumer coöperatives. It purchased and distributed to its members fertilizer, coal, twine and other farm supplies. In the seventies a serious depression wiped out jobs and drove prices up. In defense, the Grange —the Patrons of Husbandry—also organized a large number of coöperative general merchandise stores. As time went on other farm organizations, including the Farmers Alliance, American Society of Equity, the Farmers' Union, and the Farm Bureau, took to promoting coöperative purchasing. The Rochdale type of coöperative was more frequently organized. European immigrants, many of them old coöperators who settled in both the country and city, gave impetus to the growing movement.

For many years the growth of the movement was slow. In 1913 only 111 farm purchasing coöperatives were reported, with an annual total business of $6,000,000. Then came a period of increasing growth. 275 farm purchasing coöperatives were in existence by 1915 and the annual business had doubled. The next six years saw the number increased to 898, and in 1925 there were 1,217 associations with a membership of 247,000 and a combined yearly business of $135,000,000. The dollar volume of business reached its peak in 1930-1931—$215,000,000 for over 1,500 associations—but the number of associations and memberships continued to advance.

Since 1929 coöperative purchasing of farm supplies has grown more rapidly than any other form of coöperative activity. More than 50 per cent of the coöperative marketing organizations are also engaged in supply buying as a sideline. In 1933 it was estimated that 1,648 farm coöperative purchasing associations, with a membership of 542,700, were transacting an annual business of $140,500,000. The Coöperative Division of the Farm Credit Administration has tentatively estimated that farmers' purchasing coöperative associations did a business of more than $250,000,000 in 1934.

Like the farmers' purchasing coöperatives, the urban consumers' coöperatives did not make any substantial gain until the World War, when high prices brought many coöperatives into existence as self-defense measures. The years 1919 and 1920 saw the high point of coöperative interest. The last ten years have been forward years for the consumers' movement. There are now over sixty wholesale supply and insurance associations in the United States. Coöperative oil associations and credit unions—the peoples' banks—have grown tremendously.

Throughout the depression the movement gathtred strength. In 1934 it was estimated the consumers' coöperative movement was represented by 6,600 societies, with approximately 1,800,000 members, and an annual business of $365,000,000.[1] There were some 500 societies with stores, 5,300 small banks or credit societies, 1,600 farmers' supply coöperatives, about 1,500 oil societies, and 900 societies carrying on housing, restaurants, bakeries, milk supply, insurance, telephone service, medical care, electric supply, and other services. The surplus savings of the societies in 1933 were $30,000,000. The Coöperative League, formed in 1916 as the central educational

[1] "There is no complete audit of the coöperative business available, but financial statements just issued by some of the largest individual coöperative units indicate an average dollar-volume gain for 1935 exceeding 20%." From Business Week, March 28, 1936.

and promotional agency of the movement, has more than 1,450 member societies, with a total of more than 500,000 individual members, doing a business of nearly $100,000,000 a year.

Farmer coöperatives are playing an increasing part in the extension of use of electricity on American farms. They are aided in doing so by the government under the Rural Electrification Administration, set up by executive order in 1935 with an allotment of $100,000,000 provided by the Emergency Relief Appropriation Act of 1935 for the electrification of rural areas by lending money for self-liquidating projects as well as by the new Rural Electrification Act of 1936, which provides for a ten years' program with $50,000,000 made available for loans during the first year and a maximum of $40,000,000 for each of the remaining nine years.

The announced aim of the Rural Electrification Administration "is to take electricity to as many farms as possible in the shortest possible time, and to have it used in quantities sufficient to affect rural life. Power facilities to take electricity into virgin rural territory may be built by public bodies, farm coöperatives, and similar groups, as well as by private utility companies, and REA will lend the cost of such construction at low interest on a long-term amortization basis. To be eligible for REA financing a line must be demonstrably self-supporting. Preference is given to applications from public, coöperative and nonprofit groups. To help such sponsors start projects in the way which promises the greatest degree of success, REA offers the services of its staff of legal, engineering, and organization experts to advise on specific problems. Federal assistance is now available in every phase of rural electrification, making it easy for farms to use electricity for every socially desirable purpose. REA will make loans for wiring groups of farmhouses and farm buildings, for financing the purchase of electrical fixtures, appliances and farm equipment to realize electricity's benefits, and for pressure water systems, including modern kitchens and inside bathrooms."

A coöperative must satisfy the Administration as to its ability to operate the project; it must be organized so as to guarantee its continued existence for the life of the contract; its business must be conducted so as to assure payments of its obligations to REA when they fall due. "Beyond that, REA acts only as adviser on purposes and methods of operation." Coöperatives may assume all the obligations of actual operation, they may employ competent managers and maintenance men to operate the lines; or they may contract with a utility company or a municipal corporation to operate them.

The majority of rural electric supply systems in Denmark, Sweden, Czechoslovakia and Switzerland have been coöperative associations of farmers. In this country there have been some successful small electric coöperatives, but the reluctance of many private utilities to meet the growing demand for electrification in the less profitable rural areas has given impetus to the present rural electric coöperative movement, which now has a major place in the program of the Rural Electrification Administration.

An enumeration of some of the achievements of the coöperatives will picture their amazing strength and vigor. Recently 180 oil coöperatives reported to the Farm Credit Administration that their net earnings totaled $1,452,996, two-thirds of which were returned as patronage dividends. One-third of the milk of the city of Minneapolis is distributed through the Franklin Coöperative Creamery, the largest example of coöperative milk distribution in America. The retail sales for the 45 local organizations in Minnesota of the Midland Coöperative Oil Association totaled $2,439,280 in 1933. The largest wholesale coöperative store association is the Central Coöperative Wholesale of Superior, Wisconsin, with over 100 retail member associations handling principally groceries and general merchandise. The largest example of coöperative wholesale purchasing is the G. L. F. of Ithaca, New York, dealing primarily in feed, seed and fertilizer and doing an annual volume of more than $30,000,000 with over 100,000 members. The Farm Bureau Mutual Automobile Insurance Company of Columbus, Ohio, borrowed $10,-000 to get started some nine years ago. It now has assets of over $3,500,000 and is one of the ten largest mutual casualty companies in the country. The Country Life Insurance Association of Illinois made a record of $50,000,000 worth of life insurance in fifty months' time. Consumers' Coöperative Services of New York City is the largest chain of Co-operative Cafeterias in America. Although only fourteen years old it now owns 10 cafeterias, has financed a large coöperative apartment house and still has over $100,000 in the bank. The Indiana Farm Bureau Coöperative Association handles a general line of farm supplies, including petroleum products, fertilizer, farm machinery and coal. At Indianapolis is one of the three coöperative oil compounding plants now in the United States, jointly owned by the Co-operatives of Indiana, Michigan, Ohio and Pennsylvania. Farmers in 31 coöperatives in Oregon purchased coöperatively $2,009,000 worth of supplies in 1933. At the Coöperative Congress in Chicago in 1934 the National Coöperatives, Inc., the super-wholesale coöperative, took action to affiliate with the International Coöperative Wholesale Society composed of the wholesales of many countries. The ninety-first year of the existence of Rochdale consumer coöperation found 1,500 more coöperatives throughout the country in 1934 than in 1933. All over the country coöperatives are embarking upon educational programs, sponsoring coöperative schools, holding institutes and carrying the coöperative principles over the radio.

The present Administration has aided the co-operative movement in a variety of ways. One of the first measures adopted by Congress in 1933 was the Farm Credit Act in which the Administration, continuing and extending the policy of encouraging farm coöperatives and promoting their financing, provided for coöperative banks. Under the Farm Credit Administration these coöperative banks and the Federal Intermediate Credit Banks make loans to coöperative purchasing and coöperative marketing associations. It has also established a Coöperative Division which carries on researches and extends services and educational assistance.

As stated the movement among the farmers is also moving into the field of rural electrification. By the terms of an Act passed May 21, 1936, loans are authorized to be made to coöperative associations, not only for wiring, and the construction of lines, but for equipping the household and farm with electrical and plumbing appliances. Loans can also be made for the construction and operation of generating plants. Substantial progress has already been made among the states for the development of rural electrification along coöperative lines.

The law creating the Tennessee Valley Authority specifically provides for preference to coöperative organizations of citizens or farmers not organized or doing business for profit, where the Authority sells surplus power not used in its operations. The Authority has sponsored farm coöperatives for more abundant living.

In the United States the first credit union law was enacted in Massachusetts in 1909. Since then 37 states and the District of Columbia have adopted such laws. A Federal Credit Union law was enacted at the 73rd session of Congress, permitting the organization of Federal credit unions or societies— or "baby banks."

The Credit Union is growing with great rapidity. In two years' time, 1,476 Federal Credit Unions have been chartered. These unions alone in the first three months of 1936 showed an increase in members at the rate of 15,000 a month. All told there are about 5,300 Federal and State Credit Unions in operation with a total membership of 1,200,000 persons. The Unions are pure coöperatives. They make loans only to members. They make them only for useful purposes or to tide members over emergencies. They have relieved thousands of persons from loan sharks. They are operated by the members through voluntary committees and officials usually serving without salary. The present loans of the 5,300 unions are estimated at $100,000,000. There is over $3,000,-000 in paid-in stock in Federal Credit Unions while a much larger sum has been paid in on the State Credit Unions. Losses for the year 1933 were a little less than one-quarter of one per cent for the entire year for State Credit Unions. Federal Credit Unions show an even smaller percentage of loss. There are over 300 credit unions among Postal employees alone whose savings amount to $7,000,000. This is indicative of the rapidity with which coöperative banking has developed in the country and the safety with which this form of banking is carried on.

Finally there is another form of coöperative, the self-help coöperative or more properly the producer-consumer coöperative. For three years these self-help coöperatives have been organized by unemployed men and women who coöperate to produce goods for their own use and pay for them with their own labor. The Federal Emergency Relief Act gave power to the Relief Administrator to "aid in assisting coöperative self-help associations for the barter of goods and services." Soon afterward the Relief Administration set up a Division of Self-Help Coöperatives, to grant funds and aid in organizing such coöperatives. Up to August, 1934, a total of more than $1,000,000 had been granted to 147 self-help coöperatives with an active membership of about 20,000, and counting three dependents for each member nearly 80,000 people were sharing in the earnings of these coöperatives. They do many things from canning fruits and vegetables to the operation of wood yards. Only about one-half of the funds granted had then been used and the greater part of this went for tools and machines and equipment. For every dollar of the government's money spent the reports show that the coöperatives gave their members anywhere from 42c to $13.10 worth of goods and services —$2.25 on the average.

As in Denmark the agricultural side of the coöperative movement is much more advanced in our country and therefore its benefits are more clearly seen. By means of collective buying the farmers are becoming independent of local dealers and placing themselves in a better position to protect themselves against monopolistic combines, in addition to securing the advantages of large quantity purchases. Consumers' coöperatives offer many similar advantages —the return of a greater part of the profit to members, the elimination of unnecessary middlemen's profits, democratic business methods—as the Federal Trade Commission made clear in its Report on "Coöperation in Foreign Countries" in 1924. It recommended farmers' coöperative marketing and purchasing societies. It went on to say that a greater development of the coöperative credit system or credit union in rural districts would "materially promote thrift, self-help and teamwork, draw in considerable unused wealth of the countryside and make it available for credit purposes." "The distribution of electric power in rural communities," it stated, "through farmers' coöperative societies has proved so advantageous in Europe that a greater development of this means of furnishing light, heat, and power to the American farmer is recommended for the consideration of our farmers." Finally, it "recommended that the establishing of retail consumers' coöperative societies be promoted in the thickly populated rural districts of the United States." The Commission pointed out that the coöperative distribution of household coal and motor fuel has been carried on with success in a number of foreign countries; and that the coöperative distribution of milk in certain large cities of Europe, notably Basel and Belfast, had met with the well-nigh universal approval of the populace. The problem of the milk supply of Basel, in particular, had been solved by the joint action of the local consumers' society and the farmers' coöperative dairies under the supervision of the municipal authorities.

In this country the successful development of the credit union movement and the coöperative oil association and farm coöperative purchasing associations in the last few years have amply proved the wisdom of the Commission's recommendations in those respects.

Today there is more need than ever of strong consumer coöperatives to work in harmony with our producer agricultural coöperatives. It has been said that while farmers have to some degree eliminated excessive charges in purchasing their supplies with which to produce their goods, they lose much of their advantage when they reach the edge of the cities and sell to highly organized distributing agencies at the price the latter fix. Milk is often an example of the weak position of the producer before the middleman-monopoly when their real customers, the consumers, are not organized coöperatively. In Edinburgh, a city of over 350,000 population, The St. Cuthberts Coöperative, a consumers' coöperative, handles about three-quarters of the milk distribution business of the city. It pays the farmer 7c. The consumer pays 11c. In Stockholm, which is about twice the size of Edinburgh, the marketing coöperative gathers the milk and sells to the retail consumers' coöperative for 8c and it is actually retailed in bulk at 9c.

In the field of milk distribution the Coöperative Trading Company of Waukegan, Illinois, a consumers' milk coöperative was organized by a dozen women in 1910. It has since grown to more than 2,500 housewife members. It also has 38 milk producer members. It operates a pasteurization and bottling plant and more than 20 delivery trucks and wagons. In 1933 the milk producer members received $700 in dividends in addition to the regular price for their milk. The coöperative now distributes a daily average of 20,000 pounds. The consumers pay 10c but they got back in dividends 2c for each dollar for milk last year. This dividend has been as high as 10c on the dollar in the past. The coöperative has worked so well that the business has branched out into other lines and it is now doing an annual business of $800,000. The Franklin Coöperative Creamery in Minneapolis, already mentioned distributes one-third the milk of the city. It lowered the price of milk with savings for all the city consumers, without reducing the price of the producers.

Denmark is the outstanding example in the world of a country literally remade by the coöperative movement. Consumers' coöperation brought the city and country life of Finland closer together. For millions of people the patronage dividend or "divi" of the English coöperatives has meant pleasure and joy and even the necessaries of life. In Sweden it has achieved marked success in raising real wages and salaries. Coöperatives have been in a position to set the price and their lower prices have effected savings to millions of consumers without regard to their membership in the coöperative. Their prices have been used as "yardsticks" with which the public has measured the reasonableness of prices in the communities. The experience of Europe shows the coöperative to be an excellent means of obtaining the advantages of large-scale organization for small-scale farmers. Through coöperative organization the interests of producers and consumers have been harmonized. Through patronage dividends coöperatives have redistributed hundreds of millions of dollars to millions of people. During the World War the state authorities in a number of countries found in the coöperatives the best large-scale organization available for distribution of the necessaries of life and a serviceable agency for reconstruction and protecting the public against profiteers.

CHAPTER XXIX

CONCLUSION

It would be misleading to assume that conditions in America are the same as those in Denmark. Yet allowing for all of the differences, there are elemental facts as to government and as to economics that are as true of one country as they are of another. There is the same reason for the farmer to enter politics in America as there was in Denmark. There is the same necessity for home ownership; for the ending of farm tenancy; for cheap and sympathetic credit. There is the same necessity for protection from the exploiting agencies that are largely responsible for the helpless condition of the American farmer. The consequences of their power are the same in one country as they are in another.

At the root of agricultural conditions in Denmark, as in America, is the placement of power; of power that is both political and economic. And it is in this placement of power that the greatest difference exists between the farmers of America and those of Denmark. Denmark is ruled by farmers. It is ruled by producing rather than by exploiting groups. And in Denmark for sixty years there has been a progressive strengthening of the producing groups accompanied by a progressive weakening of the landed aristocracy and the commercial classes of the cities. This is the reverse of what has taken place in America. Up to the Civil War life in America was reasonably simple. There was equality of opportunity. We were an agrarian people and legislation reflected the interest of the agrarian classes. The Civil War changed this. It began the shift of power to the industrial and urban classes, a shift which has been going on ever since.

The contrast between the economic foundations of Denmark and those of America is as striking as is the political contrast. One is a mirror of the other. We have seen that in this little country of 3,600,000 people, approximately 90 per cent of those engaged in agriculture were members of coöperative societies which covered almost every activity of the farm. The turnover of the coöperatives of the country was slightly less than $500,000,000 a year, of which $395,-000,000 was in connection with producers' coöperatives. This, however, tells only a small part of the story. The various coöperatives are woven into one another; they have a common objective and a common psychology. They are in effect the equivalent of a huge, nation-wide corporation with which the vast majority of the people are in some way directly connected. It is as though the major industries of America were in large part owned and operated by

100,000,000 of our 125,000,000 people, the capital stock being distributed to them as workers, producers and consumers, and with all of the transactions open to public inspection and discussion, and dedicated to the service of the members.

Within these coöperative agencies and the control of the politics of the state is to be found an explanation of the power of the Danish farmer and his high standard of living, as in the absence of such agencies is to be found an explanation of the helplessness of the American farmer and his low standard of living. Whereas the Danish farmer, even though possessed of but a small piece of land, has complete independence in all of his relations and enjoys an economic status not greatly different from that of an industrial corporation in America, the 6,500,000 farmers of America are environed by private interests under the control of alien if not hostile groups.

The major agencies which thus environ the American farmer are:

(1) The railroads and terminal agencies connected with the railroads and closely identified with processing groups;

(2) Banking and agricultural credit;

(3) Monopoly interests in control of slaughtering, meat packing, warehousing, cold storage and marketing;

(4) The grain and commodity exchanges; and

(5) The major food monopolies which control the processing, marketing and distribution of cot-

ton and tobacco, of meat and meat products, of canning of fruit and vegetables, of poultry and poultry products and of milk and dairy products.

In Denmark these agencies are either owned by the State and consciously operated in the interest of the farmer or are in the hands of the farmers themselves through coöperative associations.

As result of this control the American farmer is all but helpless. His access to markets is in the hands of packers, commission men, speculators and buyers who determine what he shall receive for what he produces and what shall reach the market. The meat packers of Chicago and the west decide what will be paid for cattle, hogs and sheep. Commission men fix the price for perishable produce, of fruit and of vegetables. The price of poultry and eggs is determined in the same way. Only to a limited extent are the prices of farm produce fixed by the public or by a free, open market. They are fixed by speculative agencies which buy at the lowest and sell at the highest possible price.

The farmer cannot store his goods for an opportune market. He has no storage facilities. The facilities for warehousing and cold storage are in the hands of packers and commission men. Often the farmer must sell under pressure at the end of the season to pay his debts—debts which have been incurred for planting and harvesting.

Unfortunately our information as to the extent of

the control by processing groups and the cost of that control to the farmer and the consumer is very inadequate. Judging by such statistical inquiries as have been made we apparently pay enough for our food products to insure the farmer a much larger cash income than he now enjoys if he did not pay what he is compelled to pay to the processing and distribution agencies. There is a wide price spread between what the farmer receives and what the consumer pays, and in recent years, with the increase in the power of the processing groups, the farmer's share of the consumer's dollar has tended to decline. As to some products, it has already sunk to the subsistence level if it has not sunk below the cost of production.

We have some statistical data as to processing costs and the diminishing share which the farmer receives. Dr. Frederick V. Waugh, of the Bureau of Agricultural Economics, Department of Agriculture, Washington, D. C. presented the results of an inquiry in Philadelphia in December, 1933, from which address it appears that in 1929, taking the five major types of farm products of the country, comprising 78 per cent of the total value of foods consumed, the sum received by the producers amounted to $7,566,-000,000, while the total cost to the consumer was $19,021,000,000. In other words, out of every hundred dollars ultimately paid for food products, $60 went to the middle men, while $40 went to the farmers.

In the years which followed the collapse of 1929,

the farmer's share of the consumer's dollar fell rapidly. In the case of fourteen important foods in 1931 the farmer got 38¢ of the consumer's dollar, while the processors and distributors received 62¢. The following year, in 1932, the farmer received 33¢ and the processor 67¢, while at the low point in March, 1933, the farmer received but 31¢ and the processor 69¢.

Under the Agricultural Adjustment Administration and the various recovery agencies, the share of the consumer's dollar received by the farmer has been materially increased. It rose in 1933 to 36¢ out of a dollar and since that time has continued to advance.

It is obviously impossible to state with any degree of accuracy what the cost of processing and distribution is as to an individual commodity or as to farm products in the aggregate. That the processing and distribution cost is determined by monopolistic agencies interested in the highest possible profits is unquestioned. There is scarcely a farm commodity that does not pass through a monopolized bottle-neck before it reaches either the wholesale or the retail distributors. It passes through highly organized groups, conscious of their power and capable of mobilizing many agencies to their aid.

This helplessness of the farmer is much more important than the tribute taken from him by processing agencies and the acceptance of a condition in which 30,000,000 people are excluded from direct contact with the outside world and in which their income is determined for them by alien groups is in itself a denial of rights and moralities which should not be tolerated. It is not tolerated by other industrial groups; it should not be tolerated as to agriculture.

Moreover, under these conditions it is doubtful whether in the long run any gains which the farmer may otherwise make will not be taken from him by the processing and marketing groups. This is inherent in the power which these groups already enjoy. They are so well entrenched, so intimately related with one another, so closely identified with politics, transportation agencies, with commission men, with the grain and commodity exchanges, that the flow of farm produce from the farm to the ultimate market is all but completely subject to their will. It is doubtful whether any major industry could live if its access to the market were in the hands of alien agencies, whose instinct and impulse it was to pay as little as possible for the product and to charge as much as possible to the ultimate consumer.

Europe has gone much further than have we in the protection of the farmer from such agencies. It has done this by public and coöperative action. The farmer has a free access to market and this access is guarded by the state in his interest.

In almost every continental city one finds public markets. They are old institutions. Often they are located in the most prominent square in the city.

Through these markets the farmer sells directly to merchants and housewives.

Outside of England the railroads are owned by the state. They are operated as service agencies and rates and fares are consciously adjusted to agricultural needs.

In Europe the parcel post is widely used for direct marketing. Farmers have their individual customers in the towns to whom they ship poultry, eggs, and meats of various kinds. They also ship to local dealers. The parcel post rates are very low. There is little difficulty in the making of shipments. Almost every kind of commodity, of any size and weight is handled through the parcel post.

When the parcel post was inaugurated in this country it was announced as an agricultural marketing agency. It was heralded as a great boon to the farmer. It has largely failed in this respect. The postal rates are high. There are unnecessary difficulties in connection with its use. Certainly it is not encouraged as it is encouraged in Europe. The parcel post has great possibilities as an aid to the farmer. It can be converted into his own transportation agency. It can be used by coöperative societies as well as by individual farmers. By means of it he can cut through the maze of middle-men which intervene between him and the ultimate consumer.

In practically every country in Europe, with the exception of England, the slaughtering of cattle is a public rather than a private function. There is a public slaughter house in connection with every good-sized town or city. Private slaughtering is not permitted. In the larger communities the abattoirs are elaborate affairs. There are public yards for the receipt of cattle. To these yards buyers come as they come to a public market. They traffic directly with the owners or with agents of the owners rather than with a trust. All killing is by public licensed veterinaries, subject to a small charge. If the owner desires it he can have his cattle held for a favorable market or he can rent refrigeration at a nominal cost and store his slaughtered animals for sale or for personal use. There is a continuous, all the year round movement of cattle, hogs, and sheep from the farmer to the local buyers. The radio is used to keep the farmers advised as to market quotations. If prices are not favorable, animals are boarded until the price improves. There is little possibility of exploitation under this system. There is not more than one middle-man between the farmer and the ultimate consumer. This is the butcher who buys for his own use or a wholesaler who buys and kills for distribution to his customers.

But these are not the greatest gains from decentralization of slaughtering. Diversified farming is encouraged. Even the smallest farmer can raise cattle, hogs and sheep with an assurance of a nearby market and a price free from monopoly control. This diversification of agriculture provides a security not known to the average American farmer. It also assures a continuing cash income from day-to-day or month-to-month not possible under a highly commercialized agriculture. Moreover, the spread between what the farmer receives and what the consumer pays is reduced to a competitive cost sufficient to cover only such charges as are incident to the killing and storage of farm products, while transportation costs are reduced to a minimum. Cattle and hogs are not carried across a nation to be killed and then carried across the nation to be sold.

Were the American farmer provided with a local market for his cattle, hogs, sheep and poultry; if they could be brought to market at a minimum transportation cost; and if they could be killed for him at a reasonable charge and sold directly to the local market, it is possible that diversified farming might be brought back to life in this country and a substantial increase in the income of the farmer be assured.

But the problem is much more than the correction of the abuses under which the farmer now lives. For centuries he has been viewed as worthy of but little more consideration than the worker in the cities. For centuries he was a serf attached to the soil. Down to very recently he had no political rights and no social rights which those who ruled and those who owned were under any obligation to respect. This was true as to a great part of Europe down to the Great War. There are widespread vestiges of this relationship in parts of Europe today, in England, in Germany, in Poland, in the Balkans, and in all those regions where the feudal system in a modified form still exists.

The American farmer escaped this relationship for more than two centuries by virtue of the free land to be had for the asking. He moved away from the seaboard in order to be a free man. This hunger for economic freedom pushed him into the desert lands of the west and later into the cut-over lands of the central states. Finally this movement came to an end. With the passing of the free lands, tenancy began. And tenancy has recreated conditions quite as bad as those of Europe. These conditions have led to open revolt; to the entrance of trade union conditions among the share-croppers and tenant farmers. The economic collapse of 1929 accentuated these conditions as to the entire agricultural population.

The American farmer is awakening as he awakened in Denmark in the seventies and eighties of the last century. He is discovering the need of power, a power that is political no less than economic. Without the enjoyment of such power, other gains will prove illusory. They will be taken from him by other and more powerful groups, long entrenched in the government and in our economic life. And the farmer can achieve this power only through himself. It cannot be given to him by others. Even with the best of intentions those who would aid the farmer can do but little unless they are supported by the mobilized power of the farmers themselves. This means organization. It means an organization like that which has taken place in industry; like that which has taken place as to labor. Only when the 6,500,000 farmers of America are organized will they begin to realize a life of their own and a complete protection of their industry. Such power can only be obtained through the political state. It can only be gained by the farmers going into politics.

Not only must the farmer be his own statesman; he must be his own processor and his own salesman. He is almost less his own salesman than are the organized workers of the cities. Every other large-scale industry controls its product to the ultimate buyer. It is its own sales agency. Yet only as to a few products where the coöperative movement is well developed does the farmer control his product after it leaves the farm.

This, I think, is the lesson of Denmark. It is a lesson in the shifting of power. The Danish farmer got but little aid from the aristocracy or the landed gentry. He got but little assistance from the commercial or the professional classes. Even within the agricultural groups a similar struggle obtained. The Gaardemaend made war on the landed aristocracy. while the Huesmaend and agricultural workers in turn made war on the Gaardemaend. Out of this struggle a democracy emerged, and it is this democracy (rather than the implements by means of which it has been achieved), and the fruits of that democracy that constitute the lesson which Denmark offers to the world.

INDEX

A

Adult Education, 128

Agricultural High Schools, 140; practical character of, 141; curricula in, 143; value to small farmers, 144; description of, 145-148

Agriculture, low esteem of, 152; exploitation of, 153; democratic base of, 163

Agricultural Council, 161; composition and purpose of, 162

America, condition of agriculture, 179, 261; attitude toward Constitution, 188; helplessness of, 263; costs of processing and distribution, 264; Coöperative Movement in, 244; consumers' coöperation, 246; expansion of, 248; rural electrification, 249; wholesale coöperatives, 251; Farm Credit, 253; credit union law, 253; self-help coöperatives, 255; Federal Trade Commission, report on, 256; milk coöperatives, 258

Athletics, 159

B

Bacon, see Cattle Industry; Slaughtering

Banking, coöperative, 65, 75

Budget, Danish, 197

C

Capitalism, effect on initiative, 14

Cash Income, Danish farmers, 30

Caste, absence of in Denmark, 25

Cattle Industry, condition of, 89; helplessness of farmers, 90; coöperative bacon factory, 90; present extent of, 91; improvement in quality of bacon, 92; by-products, savings of, 92; high standard of, 93; unseen advantages of, 93; growth in volume, 94; English market, 94